THE THOUGHT OF CHE

D0971960

THE THOUGHT OF CHE

Editorial Capitán San Luis
La Habana, Cuba, 2016

Translation: Frances Marie Martínez Maseda
    and María Teresa Ortega Sastrigues
Design and Cover: Nuestra América
Overhaul: Jacinto Valdés-Dapena
Digital composition: Zoe Cesar Cardoso

© On the present edition:
    Editorial Capitán San Luis, 2014

© First edition: 1992
    Editorial Capitán San Luis, 2016

    ISBN: 978-959-211-324-4

Editorial Capitán San Luis, Ave. 25 no. 3406, entre 34 y 36, Playa, La Habana, Cuba.

Email: direccion@ecsanluis.rem.cu
Web: www.capitansanluis.cu
www.facebook.com/editorialcapitansanluis

Chapter 1

Ernesto Che Guevara's Ethical Thought

1. THE CUBAN REVOLUTION AND THE NEW MORAL CONSCIOUSNESS

We all know what our Rebel Army represented. And because it is so familiar to us, now and then we tend to almost disregard our emancipation epic, attained by the multitudinous thrust of the people during which twenty thousand martyrs shed their blood.

However, profound reasons made this triumph a reality. The dictatorship created the necessary ferments with its policy of oppression of the popular masses, in the attempt to uphold a regime based on privileges: the privileges of political cronies; the privileges of large landholders and parasitical entrepreneurs and those of foreign monopolies. Once the struggle began, the repression and brutality of the regime increased the people's resistance instead of decreasing it. The demoralization and brazenness of the military made the task easier and the rugged mountains in Oriente and our enemy's lack of tactical skill played a part as well.

But this war was won by the people, thanks to the action of its fighting, armed vanguard, the Rebel Army. The main weapons of this Army were *its morale and its discipline.*

Discipline and morale are the bases on which the strength of an army rests, regardless of its composition. Let us examine both terms. The morale of an army consists of two mutually complementary phases:[1] moral in the ethical sense of the word and in its heroic sense. Every armed group, in order to be perfect, must have both.

The concept of ethical morality has changed in the course of time and in keeping with ideas prevailing in a given society. To loot houses and seize all the valuables was acceptable in feudal society, but those who took women as part of the spoils of war were breaking their moral duties

---

[1] In Spanish, the same word, "moral" is used for the English "morale" and "moral".

and any army engaging in such activities as a rule would be living on the fringes of its era. In earlier periods, however, this was viewed as correct and the women of the vawquished became part of the victors' possessions.

All armies must be zealously watchful of their ethical morality as a substantial part of their structure and as an important factor in their struggle, for strengthening the soldiers.

Morale, in a heroic sense, is that fighting strength; that faith in the ultimate victory and in the justness of the cause that impels soldiers to perform extraordinary feats of courage.

Combative morale was what the Rebel Army deployed in the battles waged in mountains and plains. And that was precisely what the mercenary army lacked when confronting the guerilla tidal wave. We actually felt that powerful verse of our National Anthem: "To die for the homeland is to live." The mercenary army knew it because they sang it, however they did not actually feel the words in their inner self. The sense of justice of a cause as opposed to not knowing why one is fighting created a great difference between the soldiers of both sides.

Linking both types of morale, ethical morale and fighting morale, is a factor which makes them a harmonic whole: discipline.

There are various forms of discipline, but basically there is an inner discipline, that which is inside the individual, and another that is external. Militaristic regimes constantly work the external form of discipline. Here, we can also perceive the enormous difference between both types of armies: that of the dictatorship, exercising its morality, its external, mechanical and cold barracks discipline, and that of the guerrilla with its marked external discipline and great internal discipline, which automatically lowers the fighting morale of the first.

Why do we fight and for what purpose? For the right to uphold certain privileges of the soldiers such as their right to plunder, to receive payoffs from bookies or a cut of the profits obtained from cockfights or the right to be a uniformed petty thief? People will fight to defend those rights only to a certain point, up to the moment when they are asked to lay down their lives.

On the other side, an army with an enormous ethical morale, no external discipline but with a rigid inner discipline forged by conviction. Rebel soldiers did not drink, not because they would by punished by their superiors, but because they knew they should not drink, since their morality refrained them from driwking and their inner discipline reinforced the morality of this army that fought because they considered it their duty to give their life for a cause.

(6:317-318, 319-320)

Then comes the Cuban experience, an enriching experience because of its novel contributions, because of its vigor and energy during this period in the development of the revolution in the Americas and also because of the wealth of its teachings, which are its errors, that are publicly analyzed and corrected, always in contact with the popular masses and before the very eyes of public opinion.

Particularly important are the speeches by comrade Fidel with regards to the United Party of the Socialist Revolution (PURS) and the one on the working methods used by the Integrated Revolutionary Organizations (ORI), which represent two fundamental stages in our development. The first expresses the frank confusion of a genuine revolutionary who has reached the summit of the ascending path in the evolution on his thought, as he proclaims his Marxist-Leninist vocation to the world without hesitation. However, not as a mere oral assertion but by exhibiting the traits and the most outstanding events that prompted his evolution as a leader, as well as that of the movement and the Party, eventually leading to the creation of the United Party of the Socialist Revolution.

In analyzing himself, Comrade Fidel acknowledges a series of backward ideas that the environment instilled in him. He recounts how he instinctively fought against these conceptions and how he forged himself in the struggle. He speaks about his doubts and explains the reason for such doubts and how they were resolved.

During that stage, the 26 of July Movement was something new and very difficult to define. Fidel Castro, the hero of the attack on the Moncada barracks, and later a prisoner in Isle of Pines, trained an expeditionary force whose mission was to reach the eastern coast of Oriente, in order to ignite the revolutionary fire throughout the province, initially seperating it from the rest of the island, or to advance uncontrollably, according to objective conditions, all the way to Havana itself, through a succession of more or less bloody victories.

However, we were hit by reality: not all of the subjective conditions required for the crystallization of such an attempt were present. We had not followed all the rules of revolutionary warfare, which we later learned at the price of shedding our own blood and that of our brothers during two long years of struggle.

We were defeated and there began the most important chapter in the history of our movement. Its true force, its historical merits were proven there. We became aware of the tactical mistakes committed and that several important subjective factors were not present. The people understood the need for a change however, belief in the certainty of this possibility was lacking.

The task therefore was to create this certainty and the long process which acted as a catalyst for advancing the movement throughout the entire country began in the Sierra Maestra mountains, where endless revolutionary hurricanes, endless revolutionary fires *were ignited everywhere all over the national territory.*

Facts began to demonstrate that the Revolutionary Army, with the faith and enthusiasm of the people correctly channeled and under conditions that favored the struggle, could gradually increase its strength through the correct use of its weapons and one day destroy the enemy army.

This is one of the greatest lessons derived from our history. Before reaching victory, the correlation of forces gradually changed until they became immensely favorable to the revolutionary movement; the subjective conditions required for change had been created, which in turn sparked off the power crisis essential for this change to take place. A new revolutionary experience had appeared in the Americas which confirmed that the great truths of Marxism-Leninism are always fulfilled; namely that the mission of leaders and the party is to create the necessary conditions for seizing power and not to remain as mere spectators of the revolutionary wave growing in the midst of the people.

(36: 5-7)

What is the Cuban Revolution? Which is its ideology? And then immediately the following question always posed both by supporters and opponents: is the Cuban Revolution communist? Some will answer hopefully that it is or is moving in that direction. Others, disappointed perhaps, also believe it is; while there are those who, disappointed, think it isn't and others, more hopeful, also think it is not.

If they were to ask me if this Revolution that you have before you is a communist revolution, after offering the usual explanations in order to establish what communism is, and after leaving aside the hackneyed accusations launched by imperialism and the colonial powers that confuse everything, we would come to the conclusion that this Revolution, if it were Marxist –and note carefully that I say Marxist– would be so because it too discovered, based on its own methods, the path that Marx pointed out.

Recently Deputy Prime Minister Mikoyan, one of the prominent leaders of the Soviet Union, when toasting to the happiness of Cuban Revolution, he – who is considered a longstanding Marxist – acknowledged that here was a phenomenon that Marx had not foreseen. And then he remarked that life teaches more than the most philosophical book or the wisest thinker.

And this Cuban Revolution, untroubled by the appellatives used to define it and without bothering to know what was being said about of it, but nevertheless constantly watchful of what the Cuban people expected of it, marched forward and suddenly realized that it not only had it brought but was virtually on the way of bringing happiness to its people and that the curious stare of friends and foes alike were focused on the island, including the hopeful eyes of an entire continent and the angry glance of the king of all monopolies.

But all this did not occur overnight and allow me to tell you something drawing from my own experience, an experience that may be useful for many peoples in similar circumstances, so they may have a dynamic idea of how this contemporary revolutionary thought emerged. Because the Cuban Revolution today, albeit a continuation of, is not the same Cuban Revolution of yesteryear, even after its victory, and much less the Cuban insurrection headed by those youths, who eighty-two in all, crossed the turbulent waters of the Gulf of Mexico in a boat that sprang leaks and who arrived to the coasts of the Sierra Maestra mountains. The distance separating the representatives of today's Cuba from that period cannot be measured in years; at least not in the usual years consisting of with twenty-four hour days and sixty-minute hours. All the members of the Cuban government, though youthful in terms of age and because of their nature and illusions, have nevertheless matured in the extraordinary university of experience and in live contact with the people, their needs and hopes.

We all believed that one day we would land somewhere in Cuba and after a few cries, heroic actions and a number of casualties and demonstrations; we would seize power and overthrow the Batista dictatorship. However, history showed us that to defeat an entire government backed by an army of murderers, who besides murderers were also partners of that very government and ultimately backed by the greatest colonial force on Earth, would be much more difficult than that.

And that's how our conceptions gradually changed; and how we, who were born in the city, learned to respect the peasants and their sense of independence and loyalty; to acknowledge their age-old longing for the land that had been seized from them and to acknowledge their experience when scouting paths in the bush. And the peasants learned from us the worth of a man when he carries a gun and when this gun is ready to be shot against another man, no matter how many guns accompany that other man. The peasants taught us their wisdom and we taught them our sense of rebelliousness. And from that moment on and forever, the Cuban peasants and the Cuban rebel forces, together with the Revolutionary Government, now march as one.

But the Revolution continued to advance and we drove out the dictator's troops from the rugged slopes of the Sierra Maestra mountains. Then we were confronted with yet another Cuban reality: that of the workers, both agricultural and industrial workers. And we learned from them too and taught them that at a given moment, a well aimed shot against a person who deserves it is much more powerful and effective than the strongest and most positive of peaceful demonstrations. We in turn learned the value of organization and taught them the new worth of rebelliousness which resulted in an organized rebelliousness throughout the Cuban territory.

(10:6-9)

We accept that exceptions exist which give the Cuban Revolution its specific characteristics. It is clearly established that in every revolution there are specific factors, but it is no less established that all follow laws that society cannot violate.

Let us analyze, then, the factors of this purported exceptional character.

First, and perhaps the most important and original, is that telluric force called Fidel Castro Ruz, whose name in only a few years has attained historic proportions. The future will provide the definitive appraisal of our Prime Minister's merits, but to us they appear comparable to those of the great historic figures of Latin America.

What is exceptional about Fidel Castro's personality? Various features in his life and character make him stand out far above his comrades and followers. Fidel is a man of such tremendous personality that he would attain leadership in whatever movement he participated. It has been like that throughout his career, from his student days to the premiership of our country and as a spokesperson for the oppressed peoples of the Americas.

He has the qualities of a great leader, added to which are his personal gifts of audacity, strength, courage and an extraordinary determination always to discern the will of the people – and these have brought him the position of honor and sacrifice that he occupies today. But he has other important qualities: his ability to assimilate knowledge and experience, to understand a situation in its entirety without losing sight of the details, his immense faith in the future, and the breadth of his vision to foresee events and anticipate situations, always seeing farther and more accurately than his comrades.

With these great cardinal qualities, his capacity to unite, resisting the divisions that weaken, his ability to lead the whole people in action, his infinite love for the people, his faith in the future and his capacity to foresee it, Fidel Castro has done more than anyone in Cuba to create from nothing the present formidable apparatus of the Cuban Revolution.

(15:22-23)

It is necessary to explain what the Cuban Revolution is, what this special event is that has made the blood of the empires of the world boil and has also made the blood of the dispossessed of the world – or at least of this part of the world – boil, but with hope.

It is an agrarian, anti-feudal and anti-imperialist Revolution, transformed, by its internal evolution and by external aggressions, into a socialist Revolution and it so proclaims itself before the Americas; it is a socialist Revolution.

A socialist Revolution that took the land from those who had much and gave it to those who worked on that land as hired hands or distributed it in the form of cooperatives among other groups of persons who had no land to work, not even as hired hands.

It is a Revolution that came to power with its own army on the ruins of the army of oppression; that took possession of this power, looked about and undertook systematically to destroy all of the previous forms of the structure maintained by the dictatorship of an exploiter class over the exploited class.

It completely destroyed the army as a caste, as an institution, but not as men, except for war criminals who were shot, also in the face of public opinion of the Hemisphere and with a very clear conscience.

It is a Revolution that reaffirmed national sovereignty and, for the first time, raised the issue, for itself and for all the countries of the Americas and for all the peoples in the world, of the recovery of territories unjustly occupied by other powers.

It is a Revolution with an independent foreign policy; Cuba comes to this meeting of American States as one among many Latin American countries; it goes to the meetings of non-aligned countries as one of their important members and it sits in on the deliberations with Socialist countries and these look upon it as a brother.

It is, therefore, a Revolution with humanistic characteristics. It expresses solidarity to the oppressed peoples in the world; solidarity, Mr. Chairman, as Jose Marti also said: "A true man should feel on his cheek the blow against the cheek of any a man". And every time an imperial power subjugates a territory it is striking a blow at all the inhabitants of that territory.

(19: 54-55)

And once again, it is essential that we analyze our past life, what each of us did and how we thought as doctors or in any other function in the public health before the Revolution. We must be profoundly critical and in doing so, we will have reached the conclusion that practically everything we thought and felt at the time should be set aside and that a new type of human being must be created. And if each of us were an architect of this new type of human being, then it would be much easier to create this exponent of the new Cuba.

It is good that we stress this idea to you, people of Havana here present: the idea that a new human archetype is being forged in Cuba, which cannot be fully appreciated in the capital city, but is nevertheless present in every corner of the country.

Those of you who went to the Sierra Maestra mountains on July 26th must have observed two things never seen before: an army wielding picks and shovels; an army whose greatest source of pride is to parade on patriotic festivities in the province of Oriente bearing their picks and shovels, while their comrades in the militia paraded with their guns. But most importantly, you must have seen children who appeared to be 8 or 9 years old, judging from their physical constitution, and yet most of them are actually 13 or 14 years old. They are the most genuine children of the Sierra Maestra, the most genuine children of hunger and poverty in all its forms: they are the creatures of malnutrition.

In this small Cuba, with its four or five television channels, hundreds of radios, and practically all the advances of modern science, when these children first arrived at school during the night and saw the electric light bulbs, they cried that the stars were shining low that night. And those children, that some of you may have already seen, are learning to read and write in collective schools; they are learning a trade and the very difficult science of being a revolutionary.

And to organize this task, as in all revolutionary tasks, the participation of individuals is fundamental. The Revolution is not, as some believe, the standardization of a collective will, of collective initiatives, but precisely the opposite: it is a liberator of the individual capacity of man.

However, the Revolution does, in effect, guide this capacity. And our task today is to guide this creative capacity...

Nothing teaches an honest man more than living within a Revolution. Because none of us, none of the members of the first group who arrived as part of the *Granma* expedition, who operated in the Sierra Maestra mountains and learned to respect peasants and workers by living among them, had been a peasant or worker before.

Naturally, there were those who had been forced to work, who had faced difficult circumstances during their childhood, but none had ever felt hunger, real hunger, and we began to feel it, temporarily, during those two long years in the mountains. And many things became very clear.

We, who at the beginning strongly punished anyone who even dare touch something that belonged to a rich peasant or a large landowner, at one point herded ten thousand cattle to the Sierra and simply told the peasants,: "Eat." And for the first time in many years, they ate beef, some for the first time in their lives.

And the respect we felt for the sacrosanct concept of property over those ten thousand cows was lost in the armed struggle and we perfectly understood that the life of one human being is worth millions of times more than all the properties of the wealthiest man on Earth. And we learned it. We learned it there, we, who were not the children of the working class or of the peasantry.

And why shouldn't we shout from the rooftops, we who were the privileged ones, that we learned and that the rest of the people can learn as well? Yes, they can. Furthermore, the Revolution today demands that they learn, that they understand that more important than a good salary is the pride derived from serving your fellow man and that the gratitude of the people is much more lasting, much more enduring than all the gold that can be amassed. And doctors, in their workplace can and should amass this prized treasure, namely the gratitude of the people.

Therefore, we should begin to change our old concepts and begin to approach the people more critically. Not in the manner we approached them before, because all of you might say: "No, I am a friend of the people. I like to talk with the workers and peasants and every Sunday I go somewhere to see this and that." We have all done this.

But this was done in the form of charity and what we need to practice today is solidarity. We must not approach people and say: "We are here. We have come to grant you the benefit of our presence, to teach you with our science, to point out your mistakes, your ignorance, and your lack of basic knowledge." We must be driven by a spirit of humility, by our eagerness for knowledge, to learn from that great source of wisdom which is the people.

Many times, we will realize how wrong the notions so deeply ingrained in our minds were, which automatically became part of our rooted conceptions. We will have to change our concepts many times, not only our general, social and philosophic concepts, but at times our medical concepts as well. And we will realize that diseases are not always dealt with as they do in hospitals or large cities; we will see that a doctor must also be an agricultural worker and must to learn to plant new varieties of food; always setting an example and instilling in others the desire to consume new produce, in order to diversifying the dietary makeup of Cubans, which is so narrow and limited in a country whose agriculture has the potential to be one of the richest on Earth. We will then see that, under such circumstances, we must also become part educators, and at times mostly educators. And we will also have to be tactful. The first thing we must do is not offer our wisdom, but demonstrate that we have come to learn from the people, that we are there to carry out a great and beautiful common experience, namely that of building a new Cuba.

Many steps have been taken already, however, there is a distance from January 1, 1959 to date, and that cannot be measured with conventional means. Most of the people have long since understood that not only a dictator was overthrown but that a system was toppled as well. Now we have arrived to the moment when the people must learn that a completely new system must be built over the ruins of a collapsed system for the absolute happiness of the people.

If we all use this new weapon called solidarity, if we are all aware of our goals, if we know who the enemy is and if we know the path we must take, then we only need to know which part of the path must be treaded daily. And this is something no one can teach us since each individual must tread his own path. It is what each person must do everyday, what they will reap from their individual experience and what they will give back to society in the exercise of their profession, completely dedicated to the wellbeing of the people.

If we already have all the elements to march towards the future, let us recall the words of Jose Marti, which at the moment I am not putting into practice, but which nevertheless, we must constantly practice: "The best way to say is to do" and therefore, let us then march forward to the future of Cuba.

(11: 177-178, 181-184., 187)

This Cuban people are like this because they are in the midst of a revolution. The people have learned, while exercising their revolutionary rights during these barely twenty months of Cuban Revolution, all that has been expressed here which you, delegates from the entire world, have been able to see and experience in our country.

The first recipe for educating the people is to change the terms, to get them to join the Revolution. Never try to educate a people so that through education alone and overwhelmed by a despotic government, they learn how to conquer their rights. First of all, they must be taught how to conquer their rights and then, once the people are represented in government, they will learn everything they are taught and much more: they will become teachers and with no effort at all.

We in the Revolutionary Government, which is part of the people, have also learned these things from our positions as leaders, by always consulting the people, never apart from them, because leaders who lock themselves in ivory towers and pretend to lead the people with formulae are doomed to failure and are on the way to despotism.

People and government should always be a one and the same thing. And to the comrades visiting us from the Americas and from colonial countries that have not yet reached independence, know that it is not necessary to be cultured to lead a people; if you are all the better, if you are a philosopher or a mathematician, it's all right. But to lead a people you have to understand them and it is much easier to understand a people when you are part of that people, when you have never lived apart from the people for reasons of education or because of the barriers that separate us today.

This is why we have a government of workers, peasants and also of people who already knew how to read, but they are a minority and learned much during the struggle.

(13: 86-87)

Besides having an official Marxist-Leninist ideology, we have a practical function: that of constantly safeguarding the interests of the people, working together to improve the conditions of the people. This is why the peoples support us, over and over, notwithstanding what they may think about philosophical issues such as Marxism-Leninism or dialectic materialism.

What's important is that there is a system in Cuba which for the first time has given the people a new form of life and that this form of life has proven to be useful and usable, or at least has received the support of all the peoples of the Americas, of those who have visited Cuba. Even persons who have a very different political stance from ours have expressed their admiration for the actions carried out by the Cuban Revolution, for the concrete achievements of the Cuban Revolution...

(25:70)

But what I do know, and would like all of you to know, is that this Revolution was made with the support of the entire Cuban people and that every peasant and every worker, regardless of whether they handle a gun badly or not, is striving every day to learn how to handle it better, for the sake of defending THEIR Revolution. And if they are not able at the moment to understand the complicated mechanism of a machine because its technician left for the United States, every day they study to learn, so that THEIR factory will run better. And peasants study THEIR tractors, in order to resolve any mechanical problems that may arise, so that the fields of THEIR cooperative will yield more.

And every Cuban, those in the cities and in the countryside, moved by the identical sentiments, will continue to march forward into the future, thinking as a single unit and guided by a leader in whom they absolutely trust, because he has demonstrated in thousands of battles and on thousands of occasions his capability for sacrifice and the power and extraordinary perception of his thought. And these people, gathered here before you, affirm that even if they should disappear from the face of the Earth because of an atomic conflict; even if they were its first target; even if this island and its inhabitants were to disappear completely, they would feel completely satisfied and fulfilled if each of you, upon returning to your respective countries, would say: "Here we are. Our words are still moist from the Cuban forests. We have climbed the Sierra Maestra Mountains and have seen the break of dawn; our minds and hands are brimming with the seeds of dawn and we are ready to plant them in this land and to defend them so they may fructify."

And from all the fraternal countries in the Americas, and from our land, if it still persisted as an example, the voice of the peoples would reply, from that moment and forever: "So be it: let liberty be conquered in every corner of the Americas!"

2. ETHICS AND SOCIALIST CONSCIOUSNESS

The word *consciousness* is underlined because it is considered fundamental in the approach to this problem: Marx analyzed the liberation of humanity and viewed communism as the solution to the contradictions that caused its alienation, but as a conscious act.

It should be said that communism cannot be seen merely as the result of class contradictions in a highly developed society which can be resolved during a transition stage before reaching the summit; man is the conscious actor of history. Without this *consciousness*, which engrosses that of its social being, there cannot be communism.

(43:3)

And this is our great banner of pride, which compensates the people for all the hardships caused by the blockade, for all the threats of invasion, for all the difficulties added to those derived from the building of socialism. And in spite of everything, we continue to march on, increasingly better, despite the fact that the political situation is changeable and while the economic situation does not follow a straight, upward course; although there may be ups and downs, better and worse years, better and worst sugar cane harvests. Despite the material and specific conditions experienced during a given year, our people continue to reach increasingly higher levels of consciousness.

And our work, our work as combatants of production, is to develop conscience more and more every day throughout the course we have taken, to accomplish this in such a manner that the workers will love their factory, but they must realize that if the price for preserving their factory, their work or even their lives and those of their children intact is to fall down on their knees, this is a price that the Cuban people will never pay.

We are holding this act to celebrate the awarding of Communist Work Certificates for peaceful work, for creative work, and I do not know through which mental mechanism, we immediately started talking about shooting, about fighting and about our unwavering resolve to remain steadfast regardless of what may happen. The fact is that these concepts are very closely linked and our struggle is what enables us today to enjoy constructive peace. We aspire to maximum peace, to absolute peace, peace for all the peoples that have left the system of exploitation behind and reached higher stages of society. However, if there is anyone against repeating the Cuban reality in other peoples in the world, then it is justifiable to leave peace aside for a moment and conquer peace with our weapons.

(46: 153-154)

What does the development of conscience mean? It is something more profound than learning theory strictly from books. Theory and practice, the exercise of theory, should always go together, they can never be separated. Therefore, the development of conscience must be closely linked to study, to the study of the social and economic phenomena that guide our times and revolutionary actions, a revolutionary action that in students is equivalent to study, because it is the fundamental function of a revolutionary who is a university student, for example.

At the same time, it means searching for answers to the questions of the moment and gradually changing the attitude towards a series of fundamental problems which may affect young students. First, the attitude towards work since under capitalism, work, physical work, was considered a necessary evil that one had to do at times, however, it was also a symbol of a person's lack of capability to climb to other spheres, in other words, to those of the exploiters or, in some cases, to those of their assistants...

(30: 203)

The concepts of old society constantly weigh down on the consciousness of man. And it is here that the factors for enhancing a socialist consciousness acquire great importance.

It is not possible to reach socialism under the conditions that prevail in our country today, while many countries succeeded due to the explosion of former social conditions, in other words, as a result of a mechanical change, because so many objective conditions were present that the transit to socialism was merely a matter of form. Otherwise stated, the need for a new society had taken root in everyone's mind.

This was not the case here. In Cuba, the vanguard developed and guided the people. This was Fidel's foremost task: namely that of leading our people, always indicating what was more important, while offering them lessons in dignity, selflessness and courage as we have showed the world during these past four years of Revolution.

And that is how the people, at times moved by emotions, gradually became involved in the process of building socialism. But there are always those who fall behind and our task is not to cast them aside or to morally destroy and force them to accept an armed vanguard, but rather to educate them; to lead them forward, to get them to follow us because of the example we set or through "moral compulsion" as Fidel once referred to this. In other words, people feel compelled to do something they do not actually feel like doing, or do not feel the need to do, but are nevertheless moved by the example set by their most outstanding comrades, who everyday perform these tasks with enthusiasm, zeal and joy.

Examples, good examples and also bad examples, are very contagious and we must infect people with our good examples; we must influence the conscience of people, we must reach out to the conscience of people and show them what we are capable of doing, what a Revolution can do once in power, when it is confident of its ultimate purpose, when it has faith in the justness of its ends and in line it has followed, when it is willing, as our entire people was willing, to die before yielding an inch of our legitimate rights.

We must join all this together, we must explain until it becomes an integral part of those who have not yet understood, even of those who do not feel it as part of their inner self; to gradually convince them so that this will ultimately become a need.

(40: 49-50)

Because the peoples can accomplish enormous feats when guided by revolutionary fire, when placed in a special situation in their history, when all the small satisfactions of daily life are lost, are transformed and a qualitative change in a people entering revolution is perceived. Jose Marti referred to this as "entering revolution."

Work hours are no longer important, salaries are no longer important, cash prizes are not important. What is important is the moral satisfaction of giving part of oneself to that collective task and seeing how thanks to one's work, thanks to that small individual contribution, millions and millions of individuals come together to carry out a harmonic, collective work which is a reflection of a society that advances.

(20: 152)

A communist attitude towards life is that of indicating the path that must be followed with one's example; of guiding the masses with our own example regardless the difficulties that must be overcome along the way. Those who can exhibit the example of their work for days and days, not expecting anything from society in return save the acknowledgement of their merits as workers, as builders of the new society, have the right to demand at the hour of sacrifice. And our society can only be built on the bases of sacrifice.

(42: 241)

The problem of being a revolutionary, comrades, well, not of being a revolutionary but of assuming a revolutionary attitude, is like running 100 meters in the sense that you can be a hundred meter sprinter or a marksman or a chess player and you can have revolutionary ideas and be a revolutionary. But if you do not practice every day, you lose training and instead of running one hundred meters in 10 seconds or so, you start running them in 11 seconds and then in 12. If we do not practice our revolutionary principles, we will lose our condition as revolutionaries; we begin to coexist with errors and tend to explain why something is lacking instead of trying to resolve the problem. The system we have defended from here as an advanced system that may yield enormous results, namely that of developing a socialist consciousness, demands a leadership with a high level of consciousness.

(31: 260)

Man betters himself through education and when this education is offered with a collective spirit, when collective revolutionary surveillance contributes to the development of a collective conscience, the leap may be gigantic. We must undertake it without fear, without the least bit of fear, and without allowing any temporary failure to make us feel despondent. Time is on our side, it is there, before us, and nobody has demanded that we learn this or that in a given period of time. What we do demand, however – what we all demand from ourselves – is that we learn a little more every day. This is the spirit that must prevail.

(44: 73)

We must modify the inferior standing which stems from a lack of knowledge. We have begun the gigantic task of transforming society from one extreme to the other, in the midst of imperialist aggressions, of a blockade which is tightened every day and by completely changing our technology amidst great shortages of raw materials and foodstuffs and the massive flight of the few skilled technicians in the country. Under these conditions, we must work both seriously and persistently with the masses in order to fill-in the gaps left by the traitors and to create the skilled labor force the fast pace our development demands. That is why training occupies such a significant place in all the plans of the Revolutionary Government.

The training of active workers begins at the workplace, with an elementary education level for the purpose of eradicating the few cases of illiteracy which may exist in very remote areas of the country and including follow-up courses; later training courses for workers who have concluded third grade, elementary technical courses for workers with a higher educational level; university extension courses for turning skilled workers into sub-engineers; university courses for all types of professionals, including administrative workers. The intention of the revolutionary government is to turn our country into a large school where study and exceeding academic results are the main factors improving a persons' situation in society, from the economic and moral points of view, in keeping with their merits.

(38: 180-181)

I would now like to try to define the individual, actor in this strange and moving drama of the building of socialism, in their dual existence as unique beings and as members of society.

I think it makes the most sense to recognize his quality of incompleteness, of unfinished product. The shortcomings of the past are transposed to the present in the individual consciousness, and a continuous work is necessary to eradicate them.

The process is two-sided: on the one side, society acts through direct and indirect education; on the other, the individual undergoes a conscious process of self-education.

The new society being formed has to compete fiercely with the past. This is felt in the individual consciousness in which the residue of an education systematically oriented towards isolating the individual still weighs heavily, and also through the very character of the transitional period in which the market relationships of the past still persist. Commodities are the economic cells of capitalist society; while they exist, their effects will make themselves felt in the organization of production and, consequently, in consciousness.

In our case direct education acquires a much greater importance. The explanation is convincing because it is true; no subterfuge is needed. It is carried on by the state's educational apparatus as a function of general, technical and ideological culture through such agencies as the Ministry of Education and the party's information apparatus. Education takes hold of the masses and the new attitude tends to become a habit; the masses continue to increasingly absorb it and influence those who have not yet educated themselves. This is the indirect form of educating the masses, as powerful as the other.

But the process is a conscious one; individuals continually feel the impact of the new social power and perceive that they do not entirely measure up to its standards. Under the pressure of indirect education, they try to adjust themselves to a norm which they feel is just and which their own lack of development had prevented them from reaching theretofore. They educate themselves.

(50: 257-258, 260)

In other words, comrades, work, the focal point of human activity, in the building of socialism; work, to which today we pay indirect tribute, is also determined by its efficiency, by one's attitude towards it.

Again we have to face the past, the past which transcends the barriers where old society was destroyed and continues in the consciousness of the workers.

In this case, the past makes that daily work be reflected in the minds of many workers as an oppressive requirement, a requirement that they try to evade, as if the factory still belonged to its former owner, that is, as if they were back in the past.

And our attitude must be completely different. Work must be a moral need; work must be something we go to every morning, every afternoon or every night with renewed enthusiasm, with renewed interest. We must learn to grasp from our work that which is of interest or creative, we must learn all the secrets and every minute detail of the machine or process we work with.

If we do not like our work, we should study in order to do one we truly enjoy, so that this large part of our lives, a good part of man's life, will be something dynamic, one of its happiest moments and not one of the burdensome aspects of life.

(32: 236-237)

Today, in our Cuba, work increasingly acquires a new meaning; it is done with new happiness.

And we could invite you[1] to visit the sugarcane fields so you could see our women cutting cane with love and gracefulness, so you could see the virile strength of our workers cutting cane with love, so you could see a new attitude towards work, so you could see that it is not work that enslaves men but the fact they do not the own the means of production. And when a society reaches a certain stage in its development and is able to start a vindication struggle to destroy the power that oppresses it, to destroy its military arm and seize power, once again that former sense of elation towards work is recovered, the

---

[1] He is referring to the Spanish poet Luis Felipe, exiled in Mexico after the Republican defeat. (Editor's note)

joy of fulfilling one's duty, of feeling important and part of the social fabric, a piece of the machinery with its own characteristics – a necessary part, but not indispensable, of the productive process – and a conscious piece, a piece with its own motor which tries to propel the process more, in order to bring to fruition one of the premises of socialism: to produce enough consumer goods for the entire population.

And at the same time, together with their daily work of creating new riches for distribution to society, individual who works guided by this new attitude also perfects himself.

(46: 150-151)

However, we must mention a very serious flaw, which is the lack of consciousness, lack of revolutionary consciousness, which has not yet been completely educated.

We can say that absenteeism is the most sinister, the most subtle of all counterrevolutionaries. Absenteeism is an evil that gnaws us from within.

Many comrades have analyzed this problem and have talked in very fair terms about it, but it is good to refer to it once more. Although every day workers hear on radio and television something which has practically become a singsong: "Your machine is also your trench", etc, very fair words, a precise idea. But oftentimes, the comrades do not allow these ideas to reach their conscience. They make an excessively big division between a physical trench – the trench you dig in the ground to defend yourself from the enemy – and these production trenches.

And those who do not go to work for some trivial reasons still consider themselves revolutionary. That is why this enemy is so subtle and sinister, because if counterrevolutionaries were only ones to skip work, it would be a simple matter of statistics and according to the absenteeism index in each factory, the percentage of counterrevolution could be determined. However, the problem is not that simple, nor can we consider counterrevolutionaries those who repeatedly commit this mistake.

The problem is that there is a failing in the revolutionary level of our masses and many times there is also a failing in the political level of labor leaders and production managers, who have not been able to make the masses aware of the importance of production and the evils of absenteeism.

(22: 278-279)

Direct absenteeism occurs among people who do not feel like going to work and therefore do not go and also among those who arrive late and leave as soon as work day is over. Another form of absenteeism is that of those who leave very late and look for excuses to arrive late the following day, but who do not really perform their work well. There are those who take long coffee breaks in the morning and in the afternoon and meet with friends away from their workplace. Some have to leave the building with the pretext that the cafeteria has not yet been finished and lose an enormous amount of time, which is not accounted for and forms part of indirect production costs and still there is no one to measure it, but I can say it is considerable...

(23: 295)

The other fight we must wage is against absenteeism. Absenteeism is still in force: it is perhaps the result of having too much money and nothing to spend it on, due to the times we are living. But absenteeism is also fought with social measures, with collective measures, through discussions with the people, by offering rational explanations of the harms it causes and, all in all, comrades.

I think we have reached the moment when, if all this fails, then we should resort to compulsive measures, because we must guarantee production.

Just as a worker who steals at the workplace, who steals something from another worker, is not a true member of the working class, there are also a number of social offenses that should be tried and punished. And workers who abandon their trenches – that is, their machines — in moments of danger are not fulfilling their fundamental duty of the moment. And if there is no other way to reach out to them, if their consciousness is so narrow that they remain impervious to the criticism of their comrades; to admonitions, warnings or discussions, then let them feel it where it will hurt them most, in their own pocket; let them earn less!

(29:144)

However, we would like to emphasize the following: it is not important – nor are we seeking this – to make our enterprises profitable through the sacrifice of a few workers, nor do we intend to replace the need for labor force during a whole period of time with the sacrifice and voluntary work of some comrades.

The importance of voluntary work is not reflected directly in the economic figures contributed to the enterprise or to the state. It is reflected in the consciousness acquired through work and in the incentive and example that this attitude signifies for all the comrades at the various workplaces. That is: the vanguard volunteer workers are the most outstanding individuals, those who fully meet the ideals of a true communist, the ideals of true communists who at their workplace, in their production center – which is their place in the struggle, their trench – tell the others: "Follow me down this path." We have always insisted on this.

(42: 240-241)

And the changes that take place in the minds of the individuals give rise to a communist attitude towards work. These changes necessarily take long and we cannot hope that they will be completed in the short period of time, during which work will continue to be what it is today: a social, compulsive obligation, until it gradually becomes a social requirement. In other words, the transformation, the technological revolution will offer individuals the opportunity to do approximately what most interests them in life, in their work, in their research, in their studies of every type. And the attitude towards work will be entirely new. Every workday will be a Sunday; not the Sunday we go to cut sugarcane but a cane cutting Sunday! That is, the perception of the need for compulsory sanctions will still exist. However, in order to reach that point we must still undergo a long process and this process gradually takes place through the habits acquired while doing voluntary work, for example.

Why do we insist so much on voluntary work? Its economic significance is practically almost null. Volunteer workers who cut sugarcane – which from an economic point of view is the most important task they carry out — are not profitable. A sugarcane cutter from the Ministry cuts four or five times less than a sugarcane cutter that has done this chore all his life. But today, this task is economically important because of the labor shortage. However, what's important is that a part of the life of the individual is given to society without expecting anything in return, without any type of retribution except that of fulfilling a social duty. There it begines to be created that, which later with the advance of technology, the advance of production and of production relations, will reach a higher level and become a social requirement.

If we are all capable of combining, at all moments, our capability to transform ourselves internally by studying the new technologies and, at the same time, performing as outstanding workers, then we will certainly advance. And gradually we will become accustomed to doing productive work, something so meaningful that in time it becomes a need. Then you will automatically develop into outstanding youth leaders and you will never wonder what to do. You will simply do what seems more logical at every given moment. You will never wonder what youth will like.

(45: 77-78)

However, I would like to underline two or three things we have noticed that have not been correctly dealt with and therefore must be clarified so that the Ministry may have a unified concept regarding certain basic points that must be developed. With the emergence of socialism and the creation of the material basis for socialist development, it is necessary to insist on material incentives and moral incentives since both are closely linked. There are places where material incentives have been given more importance and this generally occurs in countries during the early stages of their revolution; when the revolutionary spirit is greater, moral incentives become more important than material incentives. Later, in general, they tend to move towards perfectly established and regulated material incentives, which in practice limit the action of moral incentives because these are pushed to a second level.

We have thought this problem over, we have discussed it and we have seen it in practice. We consider we have to fight with all our might so that moral incentives prevail over material incentives, as much as possible and during the longest time possible. In other words, we are talking about a relative process; we are not talking about the exclusion of material incentives. We are simply saying that we must strive so that moral incentives act as the determining factor of the workers' performance for the longest possible time.

We would like to propose a mixed procedure: not to hold back material incentives, but rather they should be qualitative instead of quantitative. It is the moral duty of all workers to fulfill their daily work norm.

(24: 145-146)

We have repeatedly insisted on the value of moral incentives for enhancing individual and collective consciousness as a method to advance towards socialism. Therefore, we are aware of the fact that from our positions in the central state management it is possible to exercise effective control over the industry, down to its last administrative "bolt", based on the ideological talent of our management cadres and not by resolving a series of problems through direct material incentives using priority as an argument.

It is obvious that material incentives exist during the building of socialism and we will certainly do not deny it. They will also exist under socialism. However, we give priority to educational aspects, to enhancing consciousness, and to the call of duty. And besides the call of duty, the material incentives required to mobilize the people.

The moment there is a sufficient number of consumer goods and all types of articles, material incentives will no longer be necessary, they will disappear naturally and work will be the primary duty of society. But since we know the future, and accept the future and agree that, after all, it will be the place we will reach, we have decided to start preparing conditions and to insist continuously on the call of duty; the call of duty not only for management cadres, since by their very definition they have a much more profound consciousness, but the call of duty for all the categories of production.

And when we establish our work norms, in order to set salaries – the minimum work norm, the one all workers must fulfill on a daily basis – this is actually their social duty. Not what they have to do to earn their salary, but what they have to do because it is their social duty towards the community. Through their salary, through social benefits which will increase everyday they will be able them to live, to dress, to educate their children, to acquire culture and to increasingly become fulfilled as human beings. This is a small and subtle difference; however an educational difference which always points to a well defined path and intentions

(35: 276-277)

Therefore, how can we correctly deal with material incentives? We believe we can never forget they exist, whether as a collective expression of the desire of the masses or individually, a reflection of habits from the old society on the consciousness of workers. We still do not have a clearly defined idea of how to deal with collective material incentives due to the shortcomings of the planning mechanism that prevents us from having absolute faith in this system and because we have been unable to structure a method which will allow us to avoid these difficulties. We see the greatest danger in the antagonism that arises between state administration and production enterprises, an antagonism that Soviet economist Liberman analyzed and concluded that methods for collective incentives must be replaced with other more advanced solutions, abandoning the old formula of prizes based on the fulfillment of production plans.

Although we do not agree with his emphasis on material incentives (used as a lever), we do however consider that his concern over the aberrations suffered by the concept of *"fulfillment of the plan"* throughout the years is correct. Relations between enterprises and central institutions acquire significantly contradictory forms and the methods used by the latter to reap benefits at times take on characteristics that are quite distant from the perception of socialist morality.

We believe that, to a certain extent, the possibilities for development offered by the new production relations to promote the evolution of mankind towards the *"kingdom of freedom"* are being squandered. In particular, we pointed out in our definition of the main features of the system, the interrelationship between education and the expansion of production. We can broach the task of building the new consciousness because we are faced with new forms of production relations and, although in a general historical sense, consciousness is the result of production relations, the characteristics of the present times, whose main contradiction at the world level is the existence of imperialism and socialism must be taken into account.

Socialist ideas influence the consciousness of the peoples the world over. That is why it is possible to advance the development of the productive forces to a specific stage in a given country.

The productive forces are developing, production relations change; everything awaits the direct action of the workers' state on the consciousness of the people.

With regard to material incentives, with this system we wish to prevent the lever from becoming something that compels the individual – as individuals or as a collective group of individuals – to desperately struggle with others in order to guarantee certain production or distribution conditions that will place them in privileged positions. We must ensure that the social duty of the workers becomes the fundamental element that guides their efforts, always mindful however, of the results of their weaknesses; awarding or punishing with individual or collective material incentives or disincentives when the worker or the productive center is able or unable to fulfill its social duty. Furthermore, compulsory training as an element required for promotion, when enforced nationally, will give rise to a general trend among the workers in the country to study; a trend that will not be halted by any local situation, since this endeavor will carried out throughout the country and, therefore, this will generate a considerable trend for technical improvement.

It should also be taken into account that student workers can be removed from production by means of a subvention policy, for the purpose of acquiring new skills in other types of works, so as to gradually eliminate areas where the unskilled workforce is larger, thus creating more productive factories, that is, more in keeping with the central idea of moving on to communism, to a large production society; a society where the basic needs of man have been met.

To this we must add the educational role of the Party so that the workplace will become a collective example of the hopes and concerns of the workers and the place where their wish to serve society would find an expression...

(43: 15.16; 36-37)

Those who aspire to become leaders must be able to face, or better yet, to expose themselves to the verdict of the masses and confide in the fact that they have been elected leaders, or nominated as leaders, because they are the best among the good, because of their work, their spirit of sacrifice, their constant and outstanding attitude in all the struggles the proletariat must wage daily during the building of socialism.

(40: 42)

We can now ask ourselves what a cadre is. We should say that cadres are individuals who have achieved sufficient political development to be able to interpret the extensive directives emanating from the central power, make them theirs, and convey them as orientation to the masses, while perceiving at the same time the expression by the masses of their own desires and their innermost motivations.

They are individuals of ideological and administrative discipline, who know and practice democratic centralism and who know how to evaluate the existing contradictions in this method and to utilize fully its many facets; who know how to practice in production the principle of collective discussion and to make decisions and take responsibility on their own; individuals whose loyalty is tested, and whose physical and moral courage has developed along with their ideological development in such a way that they are always willing to confront any conflict and even give their lives for the good of the revolution. Also, they are individuals capable of self-analysis, which enables them to make the necessary decisions and to exercise creative initiative in such a manner that it won't conflict with discipline.

Therefore, cadres are creative, leaders of high standing, technicians with a good political level, who by reasoning dialectically can advance their sector of production, or develop the masses from their position of political leadership.

These human beings, apparently cloaked in difficult-to-achieve virtues, are nonetheless present among the people of Cuba, and we find them daily. The essential thing is to grasp all the opportunities that there are for developing them to the maximum, for educating them, for drawing from each personality the greatest usefulness and turning it into the thing of greatest value for the nation.

The development of a cadre is achieved in everyday tasks; but the tasks should also be undertaken in a systematic manner in special schools where competent professors - examples in their turn to the student body - will encourage the most rapid ideological advancement.

In a regime that is beginning to build socialism, a cadre that does not have a high political development is unimaginable. But political development is not only learning Marxist theory. Responsibility of individuals for their acts, discipline restraining any passing weaknesses and which will not conflict with a large dose of initiative and constant concern with all the problems of the revolution should also be demanded. To develop these cadres, selective principles in the masses should be established; it is there that budding personalities, tested by sacrifice or just beginning to demonstrate their stirrings, should be found and assigned to special schools; or, in case these are not available, give them positions of greater responsibility so that they are tested in practical work.

This is how we have been finding a multitude of new cadres who have developed during these years; but their development has not been an even one, since the young comrades have had to face the reality of revolutionary creation without an adequate party orientation. Some succeeded fully, but there were many who could not completely make it and were left midway, or were simply lost in the bureaucratic labyrinth or in the temptations power brings.

To assure the triumph and the total consolidation of the revolution, we have to develop different types of cadres: political cadres who will be the base of our mass organizations and will orient them through the action of the Partido Unido de la Revolucion Socialista (United Party of the Socialist Revolution; PURS). We are already beginning to establish these bases with the national and provincial Schools of Revolutionary Instruction and with studies and study groups at all levels. We also need military cadres; to that purpose, we can utilize the selection the war made among our young combatants, since a large number of them, who are without great theoretical knowledge, but fire-tested under the most difficult conditions of the struggle, with a fully proven loyalty toward the revolutionary regime with whose birth and development they have been so intimately connected since the first guerrillas of the Sierra.

We should also develop economic cadres specifically dedicated to the difficult tasks of planning and of the organization of the socialist state in these moments of creation. It is necessary to work with the professionals, urging the youth to follow some of the more important technical careers in an effort to give science that tone of ideological enthusiasm which will guarantee accelerated development. And it is imperative to create an administrative team, which will know how to take advantage of the specific technical knowledge of others and co-ordinate and guide enterprises and other organizations of the state to bring them into step with the powerful rhythm of the revolution.

The common denominator for all is political clarity. This does not mean unthinking support to the postulates of the revolution, but a reasoned support, a great capacity for sacrifice and a capacity for dialectical analysis which will enhance the making of continuous contributions on all levels to the rich theory and practice of the Revolution. These comrades should be selected from the masses solely by application of the principle that the best will come to the fore and that the best should be given the greatest opportunities for development.

In all these situations, the function of the cadre, in spite of its being on different fronts, is the same. The cadre is the major part of the ideological motor which is the United Party of the Revolution. It is what we might call the dynamic screw of this motor; a screw as a functional part that will guarantee its correct functioning; dynamic to the extent that the cadre is not simply an upward or downward transmitter of slogans or demands, but a creator who will contribute to the development of the masses and the information of the leaders, serving as a point of contact with them. The cadre has the important mission of seeing to it that the great spirit of the Revolution is not dissipated, that it will not become dormant nor let up its rhythm. It is a sensitive position; it transmits what comes from the masses and infuses in the masses the orientation of the Party.

(33: 241-244)

Although the human individual cannot be categorized into rigid casts, where their merits are classified individually and the figures resulting from this partial classification are added to give a total sum, it can be said that factory or company directors are at their best performance when they feel in their inner self an interest for the development of the working class and of the country in general, and specifically for the success of their work place; when they establish coordination with all the revolutionary organizations and have the decision and authority to solve, under their own responsibility, all the problems that may arise; when they reach high managerial skill thus allowing them to encompass production as a whole and deal with the masses in a personal and direct way, when they are able to give orders objectively because of their knowledge, but also make others follow their example; when they are proficient in planning theory and its problems and the technology of their work place; when they have acquired a higher intellectual level and yet continue to learn continuously and consider themselves members of the working class and resort to it for experience; when they are able to leave aside the slightest personal interest; when they put law enforcement and revolutionary duties before personal friendship, when they know how to value individuals because of objective and solid facts and not because of a given aspects of their personalities or words; when they combine daring and revolutionary initiative with the greatest management discipline; when they contribute to the technical and political development of the working class by giving the workers the opportunity to study; when they have definitely learned that the great scientific truths of the revolutionary movement should be completed with constant and objective work, always taking reality into account and working armed with of theory.

Theory and practice, decision and discussion, direction and guidance, analysis and synthesis are dialectic opposites that a revolutionary manager should master.

(18: 208-209)

Revolutionary organizations gradually become the natural leaders of production because the leaders of the country are also the leaders of the revolutionary organizations and because the voice of the revolutionary organizations will provide the political tone and directly transmit to the working class, through the spokesmen of the working class who are also members of the revolutionary organizations in the factory, the slogans of the government, the slogans of the entire Cuban people.

Therefore, the importance of these revolutionary organizations, of this underlying nucleus of the United Party of the Revolution, will grow with the increase of the political consciousness of the people.

As political consciousness increases, we will also understand the importance our task has on the life of the country as a whole. We will understand, with growing clarity, how every minute devoted to collective effort, to the factory, to production, is one step more to the definitive welfare of humanity.

(22: 285-286)

They no longer travel completely alone over trackless routes toward distant desires. They follow their vanguard, consisting of the Party, the advanced workers, the vanguard who walk together with the masses and in close communion with them. The vanguard has its eyes fixed on the future and its rewards, but this is not seen as something personal. The reward is the new society in which human beings will have attained new features: the society of communists.

The road is long and full of difficulties. At times we wander from the path and must turn back; at other times we go too fast and separate ourselves from the masses; on occasions we go too slow and feel the hot breath of those treading on our heels. In our zeal as revolutionaries, we try to move ahead as fast as possible, clearing the way, but knowing we must draw our sustenance from the mass and that it can advance more rapidly only if we inspire it by our example.

(50: 261)

3. ERNESTO CHE GUEVARA'S HUMANISM

In this period of the building of socialism we can see the new man being born. His image is not yet completely finished - it never could be, since the process goes forward hand in hand with the development of new economic forms. Leaving out of consideration those whose lack of education makes them take the solitary road toward satisfying their own personal ambitions, there are those, even within this new panorama of a unified march forward, who have a tendency to remain isolated from the masses they accompany. But what is important is that others are continuing to acquire day by day a greater awareness of the need to incorporate into society and, at the same time, of their importance as the engines of society.

All of this means that for total success, a series of mechanisms, of revolutionary institutions, is needed. Fitted into the pattern of the multitudes marching towards the future is the concept of a harmonious aggregate of channels, steps, restraints, and smoothly working mechanisms which would facilitate that advance by ensuring the efficient selection of those meant to march in the vanguard and which will bestow rewards on those who fulfill their duties, and punishments on those who attempt to obstruct the development of the new society.

This institutionalization of the Revolution has not yet been achieved. We are looking for something new which will permit a perfect identification between the government and the community in its entirety, something appropriate to the special conditions of the building of socialism, while avoiding to the maximum degree a mere transplanting of the commonplaces of bourgeois democracy - like legislative chambers - into the society in formation.

Some experiments aimed at the gradual development of institutionalized forms of the Revolution have been made, but without undue haste. The greatest obstacle has been our fear lest any appearance of formality might separate us from the masses and from the individual, might make us lose sight of the ultimate and most important revolutionary aspiration, which is to see individuals liberated from their alienation.

Despite the lack of institutions, something that must be corrected gradually, the masses are now making history as a conscious aggregate of individuals fighting for the same cause. Individuals under socialism, despite their apparent standardization, are more complete; despite the lack of perfect machinery for it, their opportunities for expressing themselves and making themselves felt in society are infinitely greater.

It is still necessary to strengthen their individual and collective conscious participation in all the mechanisms of management and production, and to link this to the idea of the need for technical and ideological education, so that they see how closely interdependent these processes are and how their advancement is parallel. In this way they will reach total awareness of their social being, which is equivalent to their full fulfillment as humans, once the chains of alienation are broken.

(50: 260-261,262-263)

This is why we insist on creating everything new, that is, with individuals from the working class, from the peasantry, individuals who are a product of the Revolution. Those children who came from the Sierra Maestra and did not know what electricity was, those studying to become agricultural workers and machine operators in schools such as *Camilo Cienfuegos*, will lay the ground for new technicians, entirely united with the people and without the slightest feelings of inferiority or superiority towards anyone.

Furthermore, technicians have had their failings, but in spite of everything, and although this type of technician is not the ideal one, we rather have these technicians than none at all and in many cases, we have had to do without technicians either because there weren't any – in general, the demand for technician was much greater than those available – or because they left and continue to leave every day. It is no secret that every day an individual is bought or, and I don't want to seem unfair, they simply leave because they cannot resist the "climate" in Cuba, a new climate, and they take the path of exile, which I don't think is as easy as many believe, but these are the facts.

As a result, we have had to face a series of problems such as lack of technical know-how, technicians with little ideological consciousness which furthermore, were few. Therefore, the process of building socialism has been difficult and still is. We must resort to mass training, to the massive semi-qualification of comrades with low educational level and with them ... we must teach people to read and write quickly and once they have learned, assign them to positions they can fulfill; requiring that they at least know how to read, write and some arithmetic. But everything must be done this way. This is the great task of building. This is the miracle that a people can perform when moved by the sacred idea of production; of revitalizing their entire spirit, when they are really imbued with the idea of creating a new world under adverse conditions and at great pace, as is our case.

(16: 123-124)

We do, naturally, consider man in large masses as numbers, just as we do soldiers; one cannot have individual concerns, however when one moves down the scale, when you have to deal with people, you cannot treat them as a mere number.
To treat people like numbers is to reduce everything to very simple expressions and to create robots; and the last thing the Revolution needs is robots. It must produce individuals who are part of the Revolution, who occupy the place they belong within the Revolution...

(24:184-185)

And we are concerned not only by socialism but by the establishment for the first time in the world – and we can now say for the first time in the world without fear of sounding self-satisfied – of a consistent or almost consistent Marxist, socialist system, which places man at its center; which talks about the individual, about man and about the importance of man as an essential part of the Revolution. However, we have not been capable of developing the systems that will make man yield what he should yield and as a result of these failings in our mechanisms, we tend to turn man into a machine and even things such as voluntary work become mechanical, and voluntary work is not performed – how can I say? – does not spring from the inner self of the individual; does not grow inside the individual and bestowed on society, which is the only way work can bear fruit.

There are very beautiful words by Mao where he more or less says that: "Man as an alienated being is the slave of his own production"; a slave of work who surrenders his work and part of his nature. Man can only feel realized as a human being when he is able to do things that are not a necessity of their physical being, that is, when work becomes art, or for example, when they do voluntary work, in other words, aside from the things that man renders to society, something than man confers to society.

However, we have not yet reached the point in which man gives back to society; instead we have created an apparatus whereby society absorbs voluntary work.

I do not know if I have made myself understood with this disquisition, but these are completely different things: the need to do voluntary work moved by one's inner feelings and the need to do voluntary work because of the prevailing climate of opinion are very different things. Both must go hand in hand. The climate must contribute to make man feel the need to do voluntary work; however, if man is only moved by the prevailing climate, by moral pressures, then what is wrongly called alienation of man continues to exist. In other words, man is not doing something intimate, something new undertaken with complete freedom and therefore continues to be a slave of work. As a result, voluntary work loses much of its significance and this is something we often see. During the past days, we have seen some people wanting to know how many hours of voluntary work they have done; how many hours has so-and-so done, if they have reached the 240 hours target. We have not been capable of giving voluntary work its true meaning.

Things are not easy, but you shouldn't consider them trivial or that to talk about these things is a mere waste of time. If we are able to convey this sense to all the work we do, then we would have already taken that leap forward we are still lacking. I am sure that we can complete the framework.

There is a discipline, there are responsible cadres, serious and mature work has been accomplished in general, but a little dehumanized I would say. We must endow it with a human quality so that it will be complete, so that we can take that leap, who knows how far. And we must help the Party in this respect; we must help everyone understand these things.

We are carrying out a new experience, comrades. While looking at these skeptical faces before me, I remember the time when in the midst of a scrubland, I was forced to admonish the troops of our invading force. Men who were barefoot and starving and also highly undisciplined; with bleak, dismal faces, disobeying everything we said. At times, we even had to resort to corporal punishment to make them walk and then I told them they were writing an important page in Cuban history without them realizing it. And I believe you are in a more or less similar situation; that something very important is taking place. I can actually feel the importance of what we are doing, of the experience we are conducting and to which we are all contributing to since this is something that does not belong to anyone in particular but the result of collective work.

But there is some mental laziness when it comes to tackling the problem in depth and analyzing what we are doing and why. People are excessively disciplined in following the line yet lack conscious discipline when it comes to determining why they follow it. We must study all issues related to the building of socialism; the problems that the building of socialism entails. The problems related to the creation of a new man should be studied.

And Marx began to write about this. After Marx, little has been written on this topic, but there are materials with copious information dating from those early years, and later, in a series of capitalist materials as well. And what's more, we must incorporate the recent developments in technology. Remember something I insisted on, about this duality, about this dialectic relationship between form and content and how, under certain circumstances, it is possible to extract the form, stripping it of its capitalist content, of its idealism, of all its negative factors of exploitation. There are things that may be used, many things that may be used. We must study more...

(48: 562-564)

We must remember that machines do not, as in the capitalist system, compete with workers or enslave workers. Workers must view machines as the liberators of their force. Machines are placed at the service of workers as soon as the exploitation of man by man stops. And that is what we are striving for: we are trying to turn machines into liberating instruments of peasants, so they will have more time for leisure, so they will have more time to study, to develop in every sense, to achieve the most important thing we must achieve: individuals developed to the full, this is the aim we are all struggling for.

The future man must have a heart as simple and pure as that of the men and women of today but must also be capable of higher mental abstractions in order to make new discoveries that will place nature at the disposal of humanity, for the benefit of humanity.

(39: 36)

Because socialism, during this stage in the building of socialism and communism, is not only about making our factories shine. It is being built for integral human beings. Man must be transformed together with the advancement of production and our task would not be complete if at the same time, we only produced goods and raw materials and not human beings.

This is one of the tasks of the youths. To step-up and lead with their example the forging of the man of tomorrow and this forging and leadership includes their own betterment, because nobody is perfect and we must all improve our qualities through work, human relations, in-depth study and critical discussions. This is what transforms people.

We know this because five long years have elapsed since the triumph of our Revolution, and also seven long years from the moment when the first of us landed and sparked the final stage of the struggle. And anyone who looks back and recalls how he was seven years ago, will realize that we have covered a long, long distance, but there is still much to do.

These are the tasks and it is fundamental that the youth understand where it stands and which will be its main task. It should not pay itself undue importance. It should not consider itself the center of the entire socialist universe. It should consider itself an important link, a very important link: the link pointing to the future.

We have begun our decline, although geographically speaking; we can still say we belong to the youth. But we have endured many difficult tasks, we have been entrusted with the responsibility of leading a country in tremendously difficult moments and all this naturally ages and wears us out, and in a few years the task of those still here will be to withdraw to their winter barracks so that the new generations can take our place.

Nevertheless, I think we have fulfilled an important role with a certain degree of dignity. But our task would not be complete if we did not know when to retire. And another of the tasks before you is to forge the people who will replace us and the fact that we will have been forgotten as things of the past, becomes one of the most important tasks of the entire youth and of the entire people.

(45: 79-80)

In our society the youth and the Party play an important role. The former is especially important because it is the malleable clay from which the new man can be shaped without any of the old flaws.

The youth is treated in accordance with our aspirations. Its education is increasingly more complete and we do not forget to have them work from the start. Our scholarship students do physical work during their vacations or along with their studying. Work is a reward in some cases, a means of education in others, but never a punishment. A new generation is being born.

(50: 268)

The seriousness of today's youth in assuming great commitments, and the greatest commitment of all is the building of a socialist society, is not reflected concretely in work. There are huge weaknesses and we must strive to correct them by organizing and pointing out the sore spots; the weaknesses that must be corrected. We must also work with each of you every day, in order to clarify in your minds that the person who only thinks about the Revolution at the decisive moment of sacrifice, at the moment of combat or before an heroic adventure, that which transcends the ordinary or the daily routine; a person who is mediocre or less than mediocre in performing his work, is not a good communist. How can that be? You already bear the name Young Communists – a name that we, as the leading organization, as the leading party, still do not have; and you are the ones who must build a future where work will be the supreme dignity of man; where work will be a social duty, a pleasure in which man indulges. Work will be highly creative and everyone will be interested in their work and in that of others, in the daily advance of society. How can you, who bear that name today, look down on work with disdain?

In this regards, there is a flaw, an organizational flaw, in clarifying the nature of work and also, naturally, a human flaw. People – I think as a whole – prefer that which breaks life's monotony, which suddenly, every once in a while, makes us think about our own worth, about our worth in society…

I believe that the first thing that should characterize young communists is their pride of being young communists, an honor that compels them to exhibit their condition as young communists; a condition they do not wish to hide or circumscribe to mere formulas. Instead, they express at all moments this which stems from their spirit; which they want to exhibit because it is their crest of pride. Also, their great sense of duty, a sense of duty towards the society we are building, towards our fellow man as human beings and towards all the people in the world. This is something that must characterize young communists, who must be enormously sensitive to every problem, to all forms of injustice; as well as their spirit of nonconformity before wrongdoings, regardless of where they come from.

Furthermore, they must question what they do not understand; discuss and ask for clarification when something is not clear; declare war on formalism, on all types of formalisms; always open to new experiences, in order to adapt the great experience of humanity – which has walked down the path of socialism for many years – to the specific conditions of our country, to Cuba's reality and, each and every one of you, to think about how to gradually change this reality and how to improve it.

Young communists must always try to be first in everything. They must strive to be first, they must feel upset when they are not first in something: they must strive to improve themselves, to be first. Of course, not everyone can be first, but they must be among the first, in the vanguard, a living example, a mirror in which their comrades who are not members of the Communist Youth can look into; an example for older men and women who have lost part of their youthful enthusiasm; who have lost part of their faith in life, so when faced with this example will always react well. This is another task of young communists.

And also, a great spirit for self-sacrifice, not only when it comes to heroic feats but at all moment; always willing to help their comrades with small tasks so they fulfill their work, or help them with their school obligations, with their study, so they can improve themselves in every way. They should be always mindful of the human mass surrounding them.

In other words: young communists are expected to be essentially humane; so human that they bring out the best in human beings; so as to purify the best in human beings through work, through study, through continued solidarity with their own people and with all the peoples in the world. Their sensitivity must be developed to the maximum so they will feel anguish when a person is killed in a far-away corner in the world and excited when a new banner of freedom is hoisted in a remote corner of the world.

(34: 255-256, 258-260)

There are no frontiers in this struggle to the death. We cannot remain indifferent to what happens anywhere in the world, because a victory by any country over imperialism is our victory, just as any country's defeat is a defeat for all of us. The practice of proletarian internationalism is not only a duty for the peoples struggling for a better future, it is also an inescapable necessity.

If the imperialist enemy, the United States or any other, carries out its attack against the underdeveloped peoples and the socialist countries, elementary logic determines the need for an alliance of the underdeveloped peoples and the socialist countries. If there were no other uniting factor, the fact that we have a common enemy should be enough. Of course, these alliances cannot emerge spontaneously, without discussions, without birth pangs, which at times can be painful.

We said that each time a country is liberated this represents a defeat for the world imperialist system. But we must agree that this is not achieved by the mere act of proclaiming independence or winning an armed victory in a revolution. This occurs when imperialist economic domination over a people is brought to an end.

Therefore, it is a matter of vital interest for the socialist countries for a real break to take place. And it is our international duty, a duty determined by our guiding ideology, to contribute our efforts to make this liberation as rapid and deep-going as possible.

(49: 342-343)

We should always be ready to keep a responsive vigilance of all the peoples in the world in order to offer them our fraternal hand; to offer them our selfless assistance not only in the event of natural disasters, as occurred to the fraternal people of Chile, but also when they are fighting for their freedom, as is the case in British Guyana, to which we offered credit under conditions as advantageous as that of the most powerful country on Earth. However, they still suffer colonial oppression and those who recently seized power in Guyana refused to accept this loan.

We must also recall that the fraternal people which fought at our side during difficult times back in 1868 not only remain under imperial chains but have been transformed into an atomic base which poses a serous threat to life in that small island and that its most outstanding leader, Pedro Albizu Campos, has been condemned to a slow and tragic death in a dungeon or in a hospital that serves as a prison, for the crime of fighting for the freedom of his people.

And if I say this to you; if at this point in time I appeal to the consciousness of tobacco workers, it is to recall our duty: our duty of extending international solidarity to all suffering nations. First of all, our duty of continental solidarity to all countries in the

Americas fighting for their freedom and our duty of national solidarity to all the men and women in that country who are living under worse economic conditions than ours.

In other words, our victory today is not only a victory of tobacco workers; it is a victory of the Cuban people, a victory of the American continent and a victory of all the oppressed peoples in the world. And in occupying this advanced post, in seizing yet another trench from the enemy, we must always remember that this is a continental struggle and a world struggle and that we bear on our shoulders the enormous, difficult and glorious task of being an advanced post in the liberation of the Americas, of being one of the advanced posts in the liberation of the entire world.

(12: 197-198)

This is our responsibility. This is our strength, our duty, our obligation. This is why each task assigned to us, although it may seem forced to say it, is intimately linked to the struggle for the freedom of oppressed peoples; to the struggle of building socialism and a better world; to the struggle for a world where the division between oppressed and oppressors will definitively disappear.

This is the spirit with which we must undertake all our tasks this year; inwardly moved by the spirit of brotherly emulation, with the spirit of determination to build socialism in the shortest time possible, with the spirit of actively training for this task and with the spirit of serving, day by day, as an example for all countries fighting for their liberation, including those which still do not have the conditions required to begin the struggle.

In years to come, this will have been our great glory and this is what we must build today with our present work, with our daily work – which at times perhaps may seem dull – the work we do every day with tireless efforts although at times may seem to yield no results when it is measured from one day to the next, but whose effects may be measured in time and, also, whose effects are cumulative, because what work produces is not lost, but transformed into machinery, buildings and various facilities that are the foundations of a more rapid and increasingly serious development.

(44: 75)

Revolutionaries, the ideological motor forces of the Revolution within their Party, are consumed by their uninterrupted activity which can come to an end only with death, until the building of socialism on a world scale has been accomplished. If their revolutionary zeal is blunted when the most urgent tasks are being accomplished on a local scale and proletarian internationalism is forgotten, the revolution which they lead will cease to be an inspiring force and they sink into a comfortable lethargy which imperialism, our irreconcilable enemy, will utilize well to gain ground. Proletarian internationalism is a duty, but it is also a revolutionary requirement. That is how we educate our people.

Of course there are dangers in the present situation, and not only that of dogmatism, not only that of weakening the ties with the masses midway in the great task. There is also the danger of weaknesses people may fall into. If people think that dedicating their entire life to the revolution means that in return they should not have such worries as that their children lack certain things, or that their children's shoes are worn out, or that their family lacks something they need, the seeds of future corruption enter their minds with this reasoning.

In our case we have maintained that our children should have or should go without those things that the children of the average persons have or go without, and that our families should understand this and strive to uphold this standard. The revolution is made by human beings, but human beings must forge their revolutionary spirit day by day.

(50:270-271)

Chapter II

The Masses in Cuban Revolution

1. THE CONCEPT OF UNITY

Fidel has been aware, as usual, of the magnitude of revolutionary integrity and its greatness, since the very moment he devoted himself entirely to struggle of his people; the day he made possible the collective heroism of an entire people; of this marvelous Cuban people from which emerged the glorious Rebel Army, the continuance of the *mambi* army.[1]

This is why Fidel always likes to compare the work we have to undertake with

---

[1] Name given to the Cuban liberation army in the war for independence from Spain. (T N)

that of the handful of survivors of the already legendary *Granma* expedition. Upon abandoning the *Granma*, all individual hopes were left behind, thus marking the beginning of a struggle in which an entire people had to succeed or fail. That is why Fidel, as a result of his overpowering faith in unity and in his people, never lost heart, not even in the most difficult moments of the campaign, because he knew that the struggle was not centered or isolated in the Sierra Maestra mountains, but that the struggle was being waged throughout Cuba, wherever a man or a woman would raise the banner of dignity.

(8: 85)

We arrived at Las Villas with a flag of the 26 of July Movement; where groups from the Revolutionary Directorate, Escambray Second Front, People's Socialist Party and small cells from Organización Autentica were already there fighting against the dictatorship. An important political task had to be carried out and we understood, more clearly than ever before, that unity was a major factor in revolutionary struggle.

The 26 of July Movement, headed by the Rebel Army, had to negotiate the unity of various elements who were upset with each other and who considered that the only agglutinating agent among them was struggle in the Sierra Maestra Mountains. First, it was necessary to plan this unity, which could not be forged only with the combatant groups but also with the urban organizations. We had to undertake the very important task of classifying all the workers´ organizations in the province. This task was carried out regardless the many opponents, even within the ranks of our movement still suffering from the disease of sectarianism.

(2: 16)

But unite for what purpose? We must give the workers and peasants something that can serve as a basis for this union. In the case of the peasants, we have the magic words for this union. These magic words are Agrarian Reform. And why should the workers unite? We must offer something substantial to achieve this union. Salary increases, nationalization of public services, domestic merchant marine, full control over our subsoil...

And once this is accomplished, the Rebel Army, which is minute, but nevertheless will hand out the arms to the people to achieve these conquests. And if necessary, we will build an army of 6 million soldiers. But we must work, work, and work for that purpose.

(1:6)

We intend to have all our people marching at the same pace, with the same step; and their vanguard detachment will have to struggle and walk very quickly and with much difficulty, in order to surpass the strongest detachment, the entire detachment of the people. This is our task.

It is the obligation of the comrades of the Party to be at the forefront. Remember what Fidel told you: "The best will be there, the many Camilos, trustworthy men and women, of strong spirit and willing to sacrifice themselves." But our people will have to do what those guerrillas did, those who at first were disorganized and afraid of the enemy planes, tanks and soldiers yet, at the end, advanced throughout the Cuban territory and destroyed an army that was much more powerful and equipped with all the means of destruction but lacking morale. And at the final moment, when victory was attained, this was possible not only because the vanguard deployed great courage. Perhaps the vanguard was braver, with a little more courage, but the entire Rebel Army embodied the courage of the people.

And as their strength, their courage and their determination to fight grew, the enemy increasingly abandoned its positions, lost faith and disintegrated until it was finally dissolved.

This is our task; it is very difficult and very simple. It all depends on how we face it; on the position we assume when confronted with the revolutionary reality and on what we are able to do, devoid as much as possible of the failings of a society that is dead.

(40: 53-54)

And we must show the people that their strength lies in not believing themselves better than others; aware of their own limitations and also aware of the power of unity; in knowing that two can always push more than one and ten can push more than two and a hundred more than ten and six million more than a hundred!

(13:90-91)

When the working class united; when the peasants throughout the country united, the first step towards definite liberation had been taken, because the old, the very old imperial maxim of "divide and rule" is still today, as it was yesterday, the basis of the strategy of empires, of monopolistic empires, of economic empires.

It has been long since the Cuban people overruled disunity, long ago at least in historical terms; although this occurred following liberation, after January 1st 1959. Today we are all united; today we all know where we are heading to and we go happily and united. All of us, the honest ones, those who are used to living on a salary, those who do not aspire to live off the sweat of others.

In other words, the overwhelming majority of the Cuban people are united. But there are a few who are not only disunited but are clearly against us. They are the allies of the empire, wealthy merchants and industrialists, who every day in the shadow cast by the financial power of the United States, pick up the crumbs that the empire has left them. And that's why most of them have, and will continue to have until the end of their days, a beggar's mentality. Today they are begging for intervention, but when the imperial power tires of feeding all this rabble, you will see them begging for a piece of bread; you will see them reduced to poverty, washing dishes, desperately looking for work and that is when we must show our solidarity by offering them a hand and welcoming them as one of us.

(12: 192-193)

When the working class united; when the peasants throughout the country united, the first step towards definite liberation had been taken, because the old, the very old imperial maxim of "divide and rule" is still today, as it was yesterday, the basis of the strategy of empires, of monopolistic empires, of economic empires.

It has been long since the Cuban people overruled disunity, long ago at least in historical terms; although this occurred following liberation, after January 1st 1959. Today we are all united; today we all know where we are heading to and we go happily and united. All of us, the honest ones, those who are used to living on a salary, those who do not aspire to live off the sweat of others.

In other words, the overwhelming majority of the Cuban people are united. But there are a few who are not only disunited but are clearly against us. They are the allies of the empire, wealthy merchants and industrialists, who every day in the shadow cast by the financial power of the United States, pick up the crumbs that the empire has left them. And that's why most of them have, and will continue to have until the end of their days, a beggar's mentality. Today they are begging for intervention, but when the imperial power tires of feeding all this rabble, you will see them begging for a piece of bread; you will see them reduced to poverty, washing dishes, desperately looking for work and that is when we must show our solidarity by offering them a hand and welcoming them as one of us.

(3: 49-50)

And, furthermore, we know very well how to win; because it is possible to win, yes, by preparing conditions for the people by increasing their revolutionary awareness, by creating unity, by using our guns in the event of aggressions. This is how we can win.

Besides, in a long, vindictive war, in a war to death such as this one, you can only win by putting your shoulder to the wheel every day, by improving working conditions and producing more, by making up for the shortages imposed by the enemy with new initiatives by the people.

That is how we can achieve true, definite victory; a victory which is not merely around the corner nor will it be attained tomorrow or the day after tomorrow. It is a victory that the people will reach after long years of struggle.

This is what we must accurately specify; this is what we must instill in everyone's consciousness; to strengthen, once and for all, the awareness and the sprit of the strong and to totally weaken the soft knees of the weak so they can abandon the fight now, because it will become harder with every passing day. It will be hard in every sense; invasions have not stopped nor have incursions by pirate aircrafts. The blockade has not ended; on the contrary, it has just begun. The people will begin to suffer hardships and the best form of preventing them is with the work of each and every one of us.

But, it is necessary to recall this over and over again and to insist on it. The victory of the Cuban people cannot be won with external assistance alone, no matter how extensive and generous; no matter how large and strong the solidarity accorded to it by all peoples of the world, because the solidarity extended to Patrice Lumumba and the Congolese people by all the peoples of the world was just as big and strong, but if inner conditions fail, when rulers do not know how to hit imperialism mercilessly and when they take a step backward, they will have lost the struggle and lost it for several years – who knows how many! – but this has represented a large setback for the peoples.

This is something we must understand well: Cuba's victory does not depend on Soviet missiles or on the solidarity of the socialist world, nor does it depend on the solidarity of the entire world. Cuba's victory is the result of the unity, work and spirit of sacrifice of its people.

(14: 50-51)

2. THE REVOLUTION AND THE POWER OF THE PEOPLE

All treaties, all legal codes, all politicians in the world affirm that national political sovereignty is an idea inseparable from the notion of sovereign state, from the modern state and, if this were not so, some powers would not be forced to call their colonies "associated free states", that is, to hide colonization behind words.

The internal regime of each people, which allows them a greater or lesser degree of sovereignty, complete sovereignty or no sovereignty at all, must be a matter pertaining to that people. However, national sovereignty means, first and foremost, a country's right to be free of interference in its internal affairs, the people's right to decide the government of their choice and the way of life they consider best. This depends on the will and only on the will of that people who are the ones who can determine if they want to change the government or not. But all these concepts of political sovereignty, of national sovereignty, are unreal unless they have economic independence.

At the beginning we said that political sovereignty and economic independence go together. If a country does not have its own economy, if it is penetrated by foreign capital, it cannot be free of the tutelage of the country on which it depends and will not be able to enforce its will if the latter clashes with the great interests of the country dominating its economy.

This idea is still not completely clear in the Cuban people and it is necessary to remind them once and again. The mainstays of the political sovereignty erected on January 1st 1959 can only be totally consolidated when total economic independence is reached. And we can say that if with every passing day a measure guaranteeing our economic independence is adopted then we will be following a good path. The very moment governmental measures halt this path or withdraw, even one step, then everything will be lost and the country will inevitably return to a more or less concealed colonization system, according to the characteristics of every country and of every social moment.

We have seized political power; we have started our struggle for liberation with this power firmly in the hands of the people. The people cannot even dream of sovereignty if there is no power capable of responding to their rights and hopes. The power of the people does not only refer to the Council of Ministers, Police, Courts and all governmental institutions in the hands of the people. It also means that the economic institutions will gradually pass on to the hands of the people.

Revolutionary power, or political sovereignty, is the instrument for economic conquest and for making full national sovereignty a reality. In Cuban terms, this means that the Revolutionary Government is the instrument through which only Cubans will rule Cuba, in the full extent of the term, including its political policy and the wealth derived from our lands and industries. We cannot yet proclaim, before the graves of our martyrs, that Cuba is economically independent. It cannot be if the simple demurrage of one ship in the United States causes a factory to stop production; when a simple order issued by some of the monopolies paralyzes a work center here.

Cuba will be independent when it develops all its resources, all its natural wealth, and when assured through treaties, through trade with the entire world, that no unilateral action by any foreign power can prevent it from maintaining the pace of its production; will all its factories and land producing as much as possible in keeping with the planning system we are implementing. However, we can accurately say that the day the first step for national political sovereignty was given was the day that the power of the people prevailed, the day of the victory of the Revolution, on January 1st 1959.

This is a day that is increasingly being considered not only the beginning of an extraordinary year in Cuban history, but the beginning of a new era. And we hope that it is not only the beginning of an era in Cuba, but the beginning of a new era in the Americas. For Cuba, January 1st, 1959, is the crowning achievement of the actions carried out on July 26, 1953 and August 12, 1933, and also on February 24, 1895 and October 10, 1868. But for the Americas, it is also a glorious date, perhaps the continuation of that May 25, 1809, when Morillo rose in arms in Upper Peru, or of May 25, 1810, with the Open Town Council in Buenos Aires or of any other date marking the beginning of the struggle of the peoples in the Americas for their political independence in the early 19th century.

(8: 81-82, 83-84)

It would be unnecessary to insist in the characteristics of our Revolution, in the orig-inal form, with its dashes of spontaneity, with which the transition from a revolution of national liberation to a socialist revolution took place and in the series of stages lived at full speed in this development, led by the same people who participated in the initial epic of the Moncada, then *Granma* and culminated with the declaration of the socialist character of the Cuban Revolution. New sympathizers, cadres, organizations gradually joined the feeble organic structure of the initial movement until it became the flood of people which characterizes our Revolution.

(33: 239)

I once promised the students of this center a brief talk about my ideas regarding the role of a university. Work, a host of events, never allowed this to happen, but today I will do it, especially now, in my condition as Honorary Professor. What do I have to say to the university in the first place, regarding its essential function in the life of this new Cuba?

I must tell it to paint itself black, to paint itself mestizo, not only its students but its professors: to open its doors to the workers and peasants, to open its doors to the people because the university is not the heritage of anyone in particular. It belongs to the people of Cuba and if the people here today, whose representatives occupy all positions in the government, who rose in arms and broke the dikes of reaction, it was not because those dikes were not elastic or not intelligent enough to be elastic in order to halt with that elasticity the thrust of the people. And the triumphant people, who are even spoiled by their triumph, who are aware of their strength and knows it is overpowering, are today at the doors of the university and the university must be flexible. It must paint itself black, mestizo, worker, peasant, or otherwise it will lose its doors. The people will break them down and paint the university with the colors they believe fit.

This is the first message, the message I would have liked to convey, in the early days following victory, to the three universities in the country, but I was only able to deliver the message in the University of Santiago. And if you ask me my advice as part of the people, of the Rebel Army and as a teacher, I would say that in order to reach out to the people you must feel part of the people; you must know what the people want, what they need and how they feel.

It is necessary that we do some inner reflection and a bit of university statistics to know how many workers, how many peasants, how many persons who have to sweat eight hours a day are here in this university and then ask ourselves, resorting to self-analysis, whether this government in

Cuba today represents the will of the people or not. If the answer is affirmative, if this government truly represents the will of the people, we should then ask: where is this government which represents the will of the people to be found in this university and what does it do? And then we would see that, unfortunately, the government that today represents the overwhelming majority of Cubans has no voice in Cuban universities to issue its cry of alert, its guiding word and to express, without mediators, the will, the wishes and the sensitivity of the people.

(7: 45-47)

The socialist development and the social development of a country justly guided are undertaken for the benefit of man, not for entelechies. We are only seeking the happiness of the people and at this moment when are receiving assistance from so many places throughout the world in such a brotherly and vigorous fashion and that technology has advanced so much, there is no need to sacrifice the comforts of today for what will be achieved tomorrow.

Naturally, if there should be a very violent attack we will have to ration meat. There is no other alternative and we will ration it. However, when quality can be achieved, when quality does not replace production – we are not talking about fundamental items but of consumer goods the people need, but are not fundamental – we must make them with the best possible quality. Beauty is not at odds with the Revolution.

To manufacture an ugly device when you can make an attractive one is actually a failing. It is a failing that is constantly repeated in our country, simply because of what people commonly call "measles,"[1] because some comrades at times consider that the people must be given anything. That if you give them something bad or not good enough and not in the amount required and, furthermore, it is handed out in any old way and the people complain, then they are counterrevolutionaries. And this is false, entirely false.

The Cuban people have followed us – not followed, but rather throughout these years we have all advanced together towards our final liberation – and they have never been afraid of things as fundamental as the nuclear threats made by American warmongers. Why should we think that a people with this attitude will not be politically aware or capable

[1] Term used in the early days of the Revolution for ardent zealots. (TN)

of making great sacrifices in order to reach the end we all reckon and desire?

But it is true that the people do not like certain things that unfortunately happen and this is why we are here together today: to put an end to them. It is not good, for example, that there is soap in Havana and not in the countryside. If there is no soap in the countryside, there should not be soap in Havana. Or the soap should be distributed in such a way that there is soap in all parts.

It is not good when something is scarce somewhere and you can find it in another place; different treatment of citizens is not good in a regime where we want everyone to have the same possibilities, to receive the same treatment and to feel exactly like any other citizen, like any other comrade engaged in the great task of building socialism.

(21: 224-225)

The ideology of the Revolution, the power of the masses to carry forward the great political principles, are all based on economic achievements, on the significant and constant increase of the living standards of the population. These increases naturally do not take place every year with the same intensity and at times there must be sacrificed when reasons beyond our control demand it.

However, when a country starts a revolution, when its wealth is distributed, or redistributed, and when new wealth is generated, for the benefit of those still living below the level of the rest of the population, it is necessary to completely change the increases or historical levels of consumption; for example, the number of automobiles will not increase as before. A large part of those who could buy cars were affected by the Revolution and automobiles do not produce anything; we are not interested, after all, in having many more thousands of cars.

But trucks, for example, are indeed important. The demand for trucks will increase; the demand for tractors will increase as well as the demand for popular consumer items, which in fact has already increased as everyone knows. The demand for direct consumption agricultural produce will increase (meat, eggs, lard), of certain items such as shoes and fabrics, of certain products that are not as important, such as soft drinks, a series of items the population consumes in larger quantities when they have more money, or when they have some money, because there were people in Cuba who ate very badly and only once in a while.

Naturally, we must clarify that all this plan has been made only with the Cuban people in mind, in their aspirations to improve their living standards, in their determination to face sacrifices today in order to improve their living standards tomorrow, so everyone, not only their children, but they themselves in a few years, may enjoy a better life.

Therefore, we must also be responsible for this new continent, for this new audience which follows attentively our work every day; so that we may convince them with our example of what a country in revolution can do; a country that speaks about socialism in Spanish. We must carry out our plan, fulfill it, surpass it if possible, and raise our living standards to heights unsuspected in the Americas.

(17:171-172. 179, 188,189)

A Revolution such as ours, a people's Revolution, a Revolution made by the will of the people and for the people, can only advance if each conquest, each step is taken by the mass of the people, by the entire mass of the people. And in order to take those steps, and take them with enthusiasm, it is necessary to be familiar with the revolutionary process, to be aware of the need to take these steps and to take them gladly. And it is also necessary that we know, at all moment, why we sacrifice, why we have chosen the path of industrialization, which after all is the path leading to collective welfare in this era of economic empires. This is not an easy path. On the contrary, it is an extremely difficult path.

This leads us to an analysis, to a balance of what we have today, of what we have today from the economic and political standpoints. And we can say that we have a Revolutionary Government. I think there are few doubts that this is a Revolutionary Government; a government of the people which is deeply committed to raising the living standards of its people and creating the conditions for the happiness of the people. Furthermore, we have something that is very important, something that has not always been underlined: we destroyed the former army.

In other words, the first thing, the most important thing, was to have the representatives of the people in the government; only thus would could we truly have a government by the people. But a government must be sustained by something and that something, unfortunately, is the army, which is a necessity. Armies are parasitic entities and only ours, to a certain point, has been saved from that but, nevertheless, it is an entity that we cannot do without. And if that entity would have been the former army, then most of us, in the best of cases, would now be in La Cabaña [2]… That is, in the best of cases. This is why it is so important that the people and the army are one and that the Revolutionary Government may then advance together with the support of the Rebel Army, of the rebel armed forces, together as in one single sheaf.

(9: 127, 134)

We must fully understand that the function of the active revolutionary nucleus is not to replace administrative authority. Its mission is to mobilize the working masses and to be its vanguard organization, its engine. Its function is to control; to control plans and the behavior of managers, of everyone. How is this control exercised? There are two ways. One: In the case managers who are party members, the party is notified and, as members of the party, the individuals are held accountable for the things they are doing.

Well, that is one way: the most direct and simplest way. If the managers consider they are fulfilling their duty or if they simply refuse to

[2] A military fortress that was used as a place for imprisonment during the early years of the Revolution.

pay attention to the observations made by the party cell, the party cell can appeal to a higher instance of the organization, other than the sectional division of the ORI[3], informing it of the problems that are taking place there. The organization then sends the information here. The party cell can also call the manager's attention, if they are not members of the party cell, as in the case when managers do not respond to its suggestion, a suggestion which must be made in a brotherly fashion and not based on a method of "order and obey".

Perhaps the fact of insisting so much on these problems may seem a bit Byzantine and a little compulsory; however, they have already been the cause of many headaches. They have caused other organization an infinite number of headaches. We must put an end to them ourselves, in order to be able to work better and so that party cells can function better. We must make everyone accustomed to take their place in this process and to openly discuss with anyone, with anyone, who stated something they consider incorrect.

(27: 179-180)

---

[3] Organizaciones Revolucionarias Integradas (Integrated Revolutionary Organizations).

Comrades, the first steps have been taken: the United Party of the Revolution officially exists now in this work center. At this early stage, it is made up by 197 comrades. Which are the qualities we look for in these comrades? You know them because you were the ones who chose them. You are familiar with their spirit of sacrifice and camaraderie; their love for their country and of being among the vanguard at every moment of the struggle; their spirit of guiding with their example; of being modest leaders, leaders that do not flaunt their condition as members of the Party. But, furthermore, the members of the new Party must intimately feel the new truths throughout their entire being as something natural so that what is sacrifice for most people is merely daily action for them, something that must be done and only natural to do.

True revolutionaries, the members of the Party leading the Revolution, must work every hour, every minute of their lives during these years of hard struggle, as harsh as the one awaiting us, always with renewed interest, with increased and fresh interest. This is their fundamental quality.

This is what feeling the Revolution means. In other words, that the person is a revolutionary from within, a person who feels revolutionary from his very entrails. And then the concept of sacrifice acquires new significance.

The members of the United Party of the Revolution are Marxists; they must know about Marxism and consistently apply dialectic materialism in their analyses in order to fully understand the world.

(40: 44, 45-46)

In order to lead a revolution, to share the glory, to a greater or lesser extent, of taking part in the building of socialism from a leading position, you must be convinced of what you are doing. If not, you cannot go on. Sooner or later you will have to hand in your position to a person with more spirit. Therefore, we must work constantly and bear in mind always, first from our work desk, then deep in our heads, the fundamental ideas that must guide our work and every morning, as we begin work, to check everything, to take practical measures that will allow us to check everything and be worried throughout the entire day if your enterprise is not functioning well and insist over and over again and a thousand times, if need be, in order to correct mistakes.

(31: 258)

3. THE POPULAR MASSES AS ACTIVE PROTAGONISTS

In the history of the Cuban Revolution appeared a force with well-defined characteristics; a personage that would systematically resurface: the masses.

This multiform entity is not, as previously claimed, the sum of similar elements – reduced to the same category by the system imposed on them – behaving like a domesticated flock of sheep. It is true that it follows its leaders, principally Fidel Castro, without hesitation, but the degree to which he has won this trust depends precisely on his capacity to fully interpret the desires and aspirations of the people and on his sincere efforts to fulfill the promises made.

The masses took part in the Agrarian Reform and in the difficult undertaking of managing state enterprises; they went through the heroic experience of Bay of Pigs; they were weathered in the struggle against the counterrevolutionary groups in the mountains armed by the CIA, they lived one of the most important decisions of modern times during the Missile Crisis and today continue to work in the building socialism.

From a superficial standpoint, perhaps it might seem that those who speak of subordinating the individual to the state are right. The masses perform out with unrivaled enthusiasm and discipline the tasks set by the government, whether in the fields of economy, culture, defense or sports... The initiative almost always comes from Fidel or from the leadership of the Revolution and is explained to the people who embrace it as their own.

In other cases, local experiences are adopted by the Party and the government and made extensive following the same procedure. However, at times the state commits mistakes. When one of these mistakes occurs, a decline in the collective enthusiasm is observed caused by a quantitative drop in the contribution made by each of the elements that comprise it and work is subsequently paralyzed until it becomes almost insignificant; indicating that the moment to correct this situation has arrived. That is what happened in March of 1962 as a result of the sectarian policy imposed on the Party by Anibal Escalante.

Clearly this mechanism is not enough to insure a succession of sound measures and that a more structured connection with the masses is needed. We must improve this during the course of the coming years. But as far as the initiatives originating in the higher levels of government are concerned, at the moment we are practically using intuitive measures for sounding the general reactions to the problems.

In this respect, Fidel is a master, whose own special way of integrating with the people can be valued only when one sees him in action. At large mass rallies one can observe a sort of counterpoint between two tuning forks whose vibrations incite new responses from their interlocutor. Fidel and the masses begin to vibrate together in a dialogue of growing intensity until suddenly a climax is reached, crowned by our cry of struggle and victory.

It is difficult for someone who has not lived the experience of the Revolution to understand this close dialectical unity between the individual and the masses, where they both interrelate and, at the same time, the masses, as an aggregate of individuals, interrelate with their leaders.

(50: 255-256)

I believe that it is necessary to constantly think in terms of the masses and not of individuals, without ever losing sight of the fact that we are nothing but individuals and fervent defenders of our individuality; capable of upholding our views, over and over again if necessary, when it comes to making an analysis or an estimate of the needs of a country. It is immoral to think as individuals, because the needs of the individual are completely effaced by the needs of the human conglomerate made up by the compatriots of that individual.

(7: 111)

The building of socialism is based on the work of the masses; on the capability of the masses to better organize and lead the industries, agriculture and the entire economy of the country; on the capability of the masses to expand their knowledge every day; on the capability of the masses to incorporate all the technicians and comrades who remained in the country to work at our side in revolutionary tasks; on the capability of the masses to manufacture more products for our entire population; on the capability of the masses to envisage the future and to think it as near as we see it today – in historical dimensions and not in terms of the life span of an individual – and to embark with absolute enthusiasm along the path leading to the future.

(32: 238)

Workers, vanguard workers, today have before them a fundamental mission to accomplish: that of attracting followers with their example; of becoming revered work heroes and of creating the legend of work combatants; just like the one created around armed combatants. And this task should be carried out in such a way that it does not become completely obscure or go entirely unnoticed. It should be done in such a manner that their revolutionary enthusiasm inundates the work place, both far reaching and attracting all.

Vanguard workers should lead the masses with their example and persuasion to work. And at present, work should be a fundamental task of our people.

Today we are faced with several fundamental problems and neither work nor production alone can lead us to the new levels we aspire to. It is not possible to build socialism and create a new society through work and the production of goods alone. It is also necessary to simultaneously enhance our awareness as well as the ideological motives that make workers defend their Revolution; to make it advance so it will become an example for everyone. This task can very well be fulfilled by vanguard workers who assume an exemplary stance at the work place.

(37: 338)

And through this course, comrades, never divorced from the masses, never turning our backs on the masses, but increasingly identified with the masses, our Revolution will become stronger every day, our Revolution will be more invincible every day, our Revolution will increasingly become an example for the Americas, our Revolution will be increasingly useful and more fruitful for the hopes of humanity in its struggle for progress, in its struggle for peace. And our people will increasingly deserve the honors rendered to them.

(28: 110)

I would like to insist on our relations with the workers. We have already seen the pressing need to relate with the masses; but naturally, this is not a sin, a unilateral sin, so to say, we have committed. It is a bilateral sin. The working class is still not completely aware of its strength, of its potential, of its duties and rights.

(16: 127-128)

We believe that managers – as production leaders, as persons responsible for production, as managerial cadres – must constantly rely on the masses for support, conduct collective discussions and practice democratic centralism. They should rely on the most perfect organization of our Revolution, the United Party of the Revolution, and on the mass organizations of the working class. The United Party of the Revolution is also being restructured; however, everyday its members show more signs of activity and is currently made up by the worthiest comrades, those who deserve to represent the vanguard of the working class.

(35: 273)

Since we have dignity and a popular army, we do not ask anyone their political view about certain events; their religion and how they think. That depends on the consciousness of each individual. This is why I cannot even say which will be the attitude of the members of the Rebel Army. I hope they will fully understand the general thrust of the problem and that they will be consistent with the line of the Revolution. Perhaps they will, perhaps they won't.

But these words are not addressed to them, who represent a minority, but to the large student mass, to all those who are part of this group. I recall that several months ago I sustained a brief conversation with some of you and recommended that you remain in contact with the people. Not to approach the people in the manner of an aristocratic lady who wishes to give them a coin, the coin of knowledge or the coin of any form of assistance, but as a revolutionary member of the grand legion that rules Cuba today and to take on the practical issues of the country, issues that will also allow professionals to expand their knowledge and to combine all the interesting things learned in class with those which perhaps are much more interesting and can only be learned in the true battlefields of the great struggle for the construction of the country.

It is evident that one of the great duties of the university is to conduct its professional activities in the midst of the people and it is also evident that, in order to carry out these activities in an organized manner, the guidance and planning collaboration of a state entity directly linked to the people is required. Perhaps more than one, since currently any work undertaken in the republic usually involves three, four or more organizations and the task of planning was recently incorporated in the country, in order to avoid squandering efforts.

(4: 35-36)

At the same time, each and every one of you must think that to be a Young Communist, to be a member of the Young Communist Union, is not a grace granted by someone or a grace you confer on the Revolution or the state. The fact of belonging to the Young Communist Union must be the highest honor a youth can receive in the new society; it must be an honor they strive for every moment of their existence and, furthermore, the honor of remaining in the organization and of upholding their name high, along with the great name of the Young Communist Union, must also be a constant endeavor.

Thus we will advance even more rapidly, by becoming accustomed to think like the masses, to act in accordance with the initiatives put forth by the great initiative of the working mass along with the initiatives of our highest leaders and, at the same time, to act always as individuals, constantly mindful that our actions do not tarnish our name or that of the organization to which we belong.

(34: 249-250)

And the characteristics of our Revolution are also inherent to it. They cannot be divided from the great truths, they cannot ignore the absolute truths discovered by Marxism which were neither invented nor established as dogmas but discovered by analyzing the development of society. However, there will be conditions inherent to it alone and the members of the United Party of the Revolution must be creative, they must be able to understand theory and to generate a practice in keeping with the theory and conditions inherent to this country where we must live and fight.

In other words, the task of building socialism in Cuba should be confronted by escaping from the mechanism as if it were the black plague. The mechanism only leads to stereotyped formulas. It only leads to clandestine cells, favoritism and to a series of evils within revolutionary organizations. We must act dialectically and at the same time lean on the masses, always in contact with the masses, leading with our example, using Marxist ideology, dialectic materialism and being creative at all moment.

(40: 46-47)

The Party of the future will be intimately linked to the masses and will absorb from them the grand ideas that later will be embodied in concrete guidelines; a party that will rigidly enforce its discipline, observe the principles of democratic centralism and, at the same time, sustain permanent open discussions, criticism and self-criticism for the purpose of improving its work continuously. At this stage, it will be a Party of cadres, the best cadres, who must carry out their dynamic task of being in contact with the people, of transmitting the people's experiences to the higher instances, of transmitting to the masses the specific guidelines and of marching at their head. The cadres of our Party must be first in study, first in work, first in revolutionary enthusiasm and first at the moment of sacrifice. The cadres of our Party must be, at all moment, better, purer, and more humane than the rest.

(36: 11)

SOURCES

1959

1. Ceremony at the CTC (Cuban Workers Central Organization), January 20, 1959. *El Che en la Revolución cubana (Che in the Cuban Revolution),* Obras (Works), 7 volumes, vol. 2.

2. Social Projections of the Rebel Army, January 27, 1959. *Ernesto Che Guevara. Escritos y discursos (Ernesto Che Guevara. Writings and Speeches).* Editorial Ciencias Sociales, Havana 1977, vol. 4.

3. Speech at May Day Rally in Santiago de Cuba, May 1st, 1959. *El Che en la Revolución cubana.* Op. cit., vol. 2.

4. University reform and revolution. October 17, 1959. *Ernesto Che Guevara. Escritos y discursos.* Op. cit., vol. 4.

5. Speeches at the Auditorium in the Central University, Santa Clara, December 28, 1959. Op. cit., vol. 4.

1960

6. Morale and Discipline of Revolutionary Combatants. Undated. *El Che en la Revolución cubana. Op. cit., vol. 1.*

7. The role of university in the Cuba's economic development, March 2, 1960. *Ernesto Che Guevara. Escritos y discursos.* Op. cit., vol. 4.

8. *Political sovereignty and economic independence,* March 20, 1960. Op. cit., vol. 4

9. *Speech to the working class, June 14, 1960. Op. cit., vol. 4*

10. Speech at the inauguration of the First Congress of Latin American Youth, July 28, 1960. Op. cit., vol. 7

11. Speech at the inauguration of the Training Course in the Ministry of

Public Health, August 19, 1960. Op. cit., vol. 4.

12. Speech at the National Tobacco Plenary Meeting, September 17, 1960. Op. cit., vol. 4.

13. Words of farewell of International Voluntary Work Brigades, September 30, 1960, *Ernesto Che Guevara. Obras 1957-1967* (Ernesto Che Guevara. Works 1957-1967). Casa de las Américas, Havana, 1970, vol. 2.

1961

14. Speech at the First National Sugar Meeting, Santa Clara, March 28, 1961. *Ernesto Che Guevara. Escritos y discursos.* Op. cit., vol. 5.

15. Cuba, Historical Exception or Vanguard in the Anti-Colonial Struggle?, April 9, 1961. Op. cit. vol. 9.

16. Lecture in the cycle "Economy and Planning" at the People's University, April 30, 1961. Op. cit., vol. 5.

17.   Lecture at the training course in the Ministry of Industries, June 23, 1961, vol. 5.

18.   Collective debate: single decision and responsibility, 2nd half of July, 1961. Op. cit., vol. 5.

19.   Address to the Fifth Plenary Session of the Inter-American Economic and Social Conference in Punta del Este, Uruguay, August 8, 1961. Op. cit., vol. 9.

20.   Speech at the National University in Montevideo, August 18, 1961, op. cit., vol. 5.

21.   Speech at the First National Production Meeting, August 27, 1961. Op. cit., vol. 5.

22.   Speech at the closing of the First Production Assembly in Greater Havana, September 24, 1961. Op. cit., vol. 5.

23.   Talk with workers from the Ministry of Industries, October 6, 1961. Op. cit., vol. 5.

1962

24.   Bimonthly meeting at the Ministry of Industries, January 20, 1962, *El Che en la Revolución cubana.* Op. cit., vol. 6.

25. Televised talk on the Second People's Sugar Cane Harvest, January 27, 1962, *Ernesto Che Guevara. Escritos y discursos.* Op. cit., vol. 6.

26. Remarks to winners of Ministry of Industry study circle emulation, January 31st, 1962. Op. cit., vol. 6.

27. Bimonthly meeting at the Ministry of Industries, March 10, 1962, *El Che en la Revolución Cubana.* Op. cit., vol. 6.

28. Speech at a meeting with directors and training administrators of the consolidated enterprises and secretaries of education and work of the 25 national industrial trade unions, March 16, 1961. Op. cit., vol. 4.

29. Speech at the closing of the CTC National Council, April 15, 1962. *Ernesto Che Guevara. Escritos y discursos.* Op. cit.,, vol. 6.

30. Lecture to the students in the Technological Faculty, May 11, 1962. Op. cit., t. 6.

31. Bimonthly meeting at the Ministry of Industries, June 14, 1962, *El Che en la Revolución cubana.* Op. cit., vol. 6.

32.   Speech honoring outstanding workers, August 21, 1962, *Ernesto Che Guevara. Escritos y discursos.* Op. cit., vol. 6.

33.   The Cadres: Backbone of the Revolution, September 1962. Op. cit., vol. 6.

34.   Speech on the second anniversary of the establishment of the Union of Communist Youths, October 20, 1962. Op. cit., vol. 6.

35.   Speech on at the graduation ceremony of the Patrice Lumumba School for Administrators, December 21, 1962. Op. cit., vol. 6.

1963

36.   The Marxist-Leninist Party, 1963. Op. cit., vol. 7.

37.   Speech honoring the most outstanding workers in 1962, January 27, 1963, *El Che en la Revolución cubana.* Op. cit., vol. 4.

38. Against Bureaucratism, February 1963, *Ernesto Che Guevara. Obras 1957-1967*. Op. cit., vol. 2.

39. Speech at the National Sugar Plenary Meeting in Camagüey, Febrary 9, 1963 *Ernesto Che Guevara. Escritos y discursos*. Op. cit., vol. 7.

40. Speech at the General Assembly of the workers in Ariguanabo Textile Factory, March 24, 1963. Op. cit., vol. 7.

41. Closing speech at the First International Meeting of Architecture Teachers and Students, September 29, 1963. Op. cit., vol. 7.

1964

42. Speech at ceremony awarding Certificates of Communist Work, January 11, 1964. *Ernesto Che Guevara. Obras 1957-1967*. Op. cit., vol. 2.

43. On Budgetary Finance System. February 1964, *Ernesto Che Guevara. Escritos y discursos*. Op. cit., vol. 8.

44. Speech honoring winners of national emulation in the Ministry of Industries, March 14, 1964,

El Che en la Revolución cubana.
Op. cit., vol. 5.

45. Speech at the Ministry of Industries,
May 9, 1964, *Ernesto Che Guevara.
Escritos y discursos.* Op. cit., vol. 8.

46. Speech at ceremony awarding
Certificates for Communist Work at
the Ministry of Industries, August 15,
1964. Op. cit., vol. 8.

47. Speech at the Socialist Emulation
Assembly of the Ministry of Industries,
October 22, 1964. Op. cit., vol. 8.

48. Bimonthly meeting at the Ministry of
Industries, December 5, 1964, *El Che en
la Revolución cubana.* Op. cit., vol. 6.

1965

49. Address to the Second Economic
Seminar of Afro-Asian Solidarity in
Algeria, February 24, 1965. *Ernesto
Che Guevara. Escritos y discursos.*
Op. cit., vol. 9.

50. *Socialism and Man in Cuba,* March 12,
1965. Op. cit., vol. 8.

Indice